The Mountains o' Mourne.

A PICTURE OF PERCY FRENCH

A PICTURE OF

Percy French

by Alan Tongue

An illustrated life of the Irish
Songwriter, Entertainer, Poet and Painter

GREYSTONE
BOOKS

To Ettie and Joan French.

*Pencil sketch by Raymond Piper of Ettie French, on the right, and
Joan French, daughters of Percy French.*

© Alan Tongue 1990

First published 1990 by Greystone Books Ltd.
in association with the Percy French Society.
(who acknowledge the assistance of the Ireland Fund)
Reprinted 1991

ISBN 1 870157 11 7

Designed by: Rodney Miller Associates, Belfast.
Printed by: W. & G. Baird Ltd., Antrim.

FOREWORD
BY ETTIE FRENCH

This picture book deserves a special welcome because it emphasises for the first time the primary importance of landscape painting in Percy French's life. Even those shown in Alan Tongue's highly successful TV documentary, 'Percy French Remembered', could not make as strong an impact as the beautifully reproduced examples shown here. For the rest, Alan allows his subject to speak for himself in poems and prose, not forgetting the scrap of autobiography with its revealing touch of the author's character.

Willie French (Willie to all his friends and not yet dubbed Percy by his agents) was thirty when he was first attracted to landscape painting. He was enjoying a life full of congenial activities (see 'Red-Letter Days' on p.61) and deeply in love with the girl he was going to marry, when a series of wonderful sunsets over Lough Sheelin completely bowled him over. He went out every evening and tried to capture in paint the colours, which were due to volcanic dust. After that he sketched wherever he went, from the Fall in Canada to the bright colours and blue distances of the Jamaican summer. Later in Switzerland he solved the problem of painting the beautiful afterglow with a bottle of Indian ink. But every year after a busy London season as an entertainer, followed by a hectic month long tour of the Irish seaside resorts, he insisted on spending four weeks of perfect freedom on his own in the west of Ireland, refreshing his memory of the scenes he loved. This break was an absolute lifeline – his poem 'To the West' tells it all. Alan's share in the text of the picture book gives a finishing touch to years of research and travel to find material for it and for a host of other activities that include the organisation of the first public exhibition of Percy French's pictures for many years. With his last two achievements of the documentary and picture book, Alan can rest on his laurels as an outstanding contributor to our knowledge and appreciation of a very remarkable man.

Ettie Percy French

AUTHOR'S NOTE

I had just finished recording a radio programme with Brendan O'Dowda on the songs of Percy French in a small hall in Newcastle, County Down ('*Where the Mountains o' Mourne sweep down to the sea*') when two ladies stepped up out of the audience. Ettie and Joan French, the songwriter's daughters, had been on holiday in the region and seen a poster advertising the show. That was my first meeting with the French family. Since then I have spent many happy times talking with them in their delightful home in Suffolk and also helped them unearth their treasure trove of memorabilia about their father's life.

After my film documentary on Percy French, Ettie told me that the reaction she had from viewers who wrote to her was that Percy French was a person they would have liked to have known. In this book I have tried to let him tell his own story. For the text of the poems I have sometimes used versions earlier than those in the collection edited by his sister after his death: I believe these earlier texts are more in character, and they are without the misprints that crept in later.

As well as thanking Ettie and Joan French, the other members of the family that have given me much help are Courtney Kenny, Maeve Kenny, Daphne French, Clare French and Phyllis Killingley. I thank them all for their continual encouragement. I am grateful to Brendan O'Dowda for kindling my interest in Percy French in the first place, to James N. Healy for much assistance along the way, and to the Percy French Society for their determination to have this book published, especially Ann Gibson, Oscar Rollins and Berry O'Neill. For help with details of research I am grateful to many people, but particularly Derek Collie, Pat Nally in Cavan, and Tom Turpin in T.C.D. Others who have given useful assistance over the years include Colette Roberts, Henry McIlhenny, Oliver Nulty, Brian O'Carroll, Neil Shawcross, Phyllis Arnold, Alan Roberts, John Petrie, The Bodleian Library, the BBC, the British Library, Central Library (Belfast), The Law Society, McCullough-Pigott, National Gallery of Ireland, The National Library of Ireland, North Down Heritage Centre, The Queen's University of Belfast, Ulster Folk Museum, Ulster Museum, Trinity College, Dublin, and of course the Percy French Society.

Alan Tongue
September 1990

CONTENTS

CHAPTER ONE:

CLOONYQUIN

William Percy French was born at Cloonyquin, County Roscommon, on May Day, 1st May 1854.

RETROSPECTION

A boat upon the billow
A bird upon the wing
A boy upon a bicycle
Sailing through the Spring.

List'ning in the greenwood
For redskins in the scrub
Cows – a herd of buffaloes!
The cat – a tiger cub!

The lonely curlew calling
Meant a maiden in despair,
And the rustling of the rabbit
Was the advent of a bear.

•   •   •   •   •

Could I find again the woodland
Where I loved to lie and dream,
While the dragonflies were dancing
To the rippling of the stream.

I'd give up all the world has brought
And all that it may bring,
To be that merry boy again
Sailing through the Spring.

Nearly sixty years ago an event of immense importance occurred in the history of Ireland. No cables buzzed the news to the ends of the earth. No telephones rang – there were none to ring. Cabinets were not hastily summoned nor consuls recalled, but Larry McCullough lepped on the 'chistnut mare' and galloped as fasht as he could shplit for Dr. Peyton. By the time the doctor arrived I was an accomplished fact, endowed by my parents with all the mental activity of the house of French and all the physical health and beauty of the Percys.

Tutors and governesses came at intervals out of space and taught me little except that all learning was a fearful bore – in fact, it was not until after I left college that I began to take any pleasure in working my brains.

My old friend and tutor, the Rev. James Rountree, was the first man to show me that 'two straight lines cannot enclose a space – unless one of them is crooked' (he's Irish, is friend James!) and as he taught me Euclid with a rule and compass I really got a practical knowledge of the first book. When my family migrated to Derby for educational purposes, and I was sent to a small school called Kirk Langley, none of the boys had as yet attempted Euclid. I was accordingly hailed as a prodigy, and the headmaster, Dr. Barton, wrote home to my father in these words: 'Your son, for his age, is quite the finest mathematical scholar we have ever had!' This fatal remark exercised a most baleful influence over my whole life.

Still a victim to the 'great mathematician' myth, I was sent to Windermere College, as the headmaster, George Puckle, had published a book on Conic Sections and kindred spoil sports. I never got to know what Conic Sections were, or what they did, but in my second term I was champion fives player of the lower school. Just before I entered Trinity College I was sent to Foyle College, where an eminent mathematician named Johnson was requested to put in the finishing touch. He built up a beautiful superstructure on the flimsiest foundation, and I passed into TCD with honours!

Foyle College mathematics prize, 1872

Jeffrey French
of Mulpit, Co. Galway

|

Christopher French
of Mulpit & Tyrone, Co. Galway
m. Jane

|

Arthur French
of Tyrone, Co. Galway, & Cloonyquin
m. Sarah Burke 1691

|

Arthur French
of Cloonyquin, High Sheriff
m. Judith Davis 1715

|

Christopher French
c. 1725-1797
m. Margarita Alberti 1748

|

John French
of Cloonyquin
1764-1823
m. Ann Story 1789

|

William Christopher St. George French
of Cloonyquin, High Sheriff
1790-1852
m. Dorothea Helen Harris 1819

|

Christopher French
of Cloonyquin, J.P., D.L., High Sheriff
1821-1897
m. Susan Emma Percy 1851

| Elizabeth Jane b.1851 | Arthur John St. George b.1853 | **William Percy** b.1854 | Dorothea Emma b.1855 | Alice Kathleen b.1857 | Emily Lucy b.1859 | Henry Percy b.1863 | Christine Laura Sophie b.1869 | Christopher St. George b.1872 |

French entered Trinity College, Dublin, in October 1872 to study Engineering. A year later he transferred to Arts, gaining his B.A. degree in the winter of 1876, and finally his B.Eng. degree in the summer of 1881.

Here was a chance to learn everything! Lectures by Specialists of world-wide fame, a magnificent library, quiet rooms in the new square, debating societies, aspiring students all around me – yet nothing I wanted to know. Oh yes, there was! The Gaiety Theatre had just been opened, and Miss Annie Tremaine and Company were playing Offenbach's operas! Night after night I was in the pit marching to battle with General Boom, or listening to the poor little Perichole bidding her lover good-bye. 'Music held me with its magic spell' – so I bought a banjo.

The Museum Building, T.C.D.

French (with banjo) and his cousin Johnny Richardson.

I believe I still hold the record as the student who took the longest time to get the C.E. degree. Bright-eyed boys would pass through the school and get lucrative posts in various parts of the world, returning years after bronzed and bearded men to find me still attending Apjohn's lectures on the Skew Arch! I think taking up the banjo, lawn tennis, and water-colour painting, instead of Chemistry, Geology and the theory of strains, must have retarded my progress a good deal. But eventually I was allowed to take out my B.A. and C.E. degrees – I believe the Board were afraid I should apply for a pension if I stayed any longer in T.C.D.

My only contribution to contemporary literature during my college career was a ballad called '*Abdallah Bulbul Ameer*'. It described a duel betweeen a Turk and a Russian during the Russo-Turkish War, and became so popular at college smokers that I determined to publish it. To borrow a fiver from Archie West, the only man of means in my class, was the work of a moment, and when Messrs Cramer and Co. handed me 200 copies to be disposed of at 1s. 6d. a copy, Eldorado seemed round the corner. But alas! we had forgotten to take out the copyright, and a London firm, finding out our mistake, brought out a pirated edition without even my name on the cover! As they had taken care to copyright *their* version, I was tricked out of all rights to my song, though words and music were both mine.

Oh, the sons of the Prophet are hardy and grim
And quite unaccustomed to fear
But none were so reckless of life or of limb
As Abdallah Bulbul Ameer.
When they wanted a man to encourage the van
Or to harrass the foe in the rear
Or to take a redoubt they would always send out
For Abdallah Bulbul Ameer.

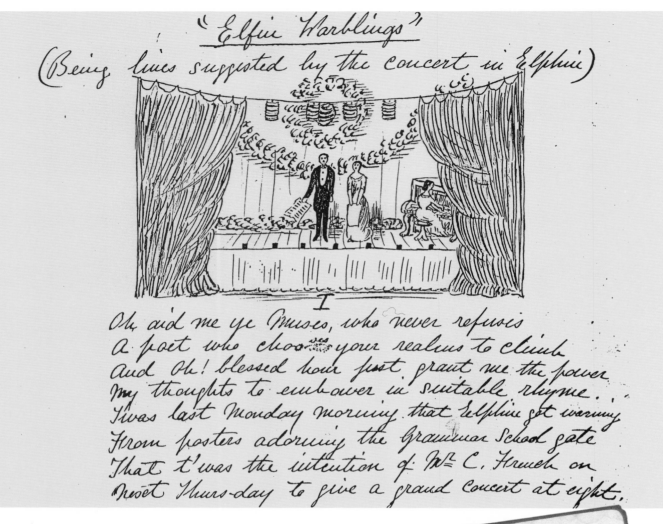

"Elfin Warblings"
(Being lines suggested by the concert in Elphin)

I

Oh aid me ye Muses, who never refuses
A poet who choose your realms to climb
And Oh! blessed hour just grant me the power
My thoughts to embower in suitable rhyme.
'Twas last Monday morning that Elphin got warning
From posters adorning the Grammar School gate
That t'was the intention of Mrs C. French on
Next Thurs-day to give a grand concert at eight.

From the 1874 Christmas edition of **The Trombone of Truth,** *a family magazine edited by French with help from his sisters, cousins and friends, especially A. D. Godley, just then setting out on a distinguished career at Oxford University. (French is on the right.)*

Sambo, alias French.

Having taken out my C.E. I sat down to await letters from Sir Thomas Brassey, Sir Hiram Maxim, and Sir James Bessemer asking me to take over their concerns and remodel them at my own terms. As none of them seemed to be able to find my address, I put in the time as an apprentice under James Price, Engineer-in-Chief of the Midland Railway.

It was when working under James Price – there was no work but none of us grumbled – that I made my first appearance in public. My companion-in-crime was no less a personage than Charles Manners. Charles was also an apprentice, and during office hours we rehearsed duets together – I was wrong when I said we did no work – chiefly negro melodies with a banjo and bones accompaniment.

Punchestown Races were close at hand, and it seemed a fine idea to the Manners-French combine to go down to the racecourse, where we had no doubt our concerted music would bring us in much gold. The crowd soon found out we weren't 'funny' men, and knew no music hall songs. The carriage folk wouldn't let us begin, as they took it for granted we were 'quite too vulgar for anything.' Soon we were washing the burnt cork off our faces in a muddy stream and found, after paying our fares home, we had 8d. to divide! That eminent grinder Marmaduke Backhouse who, when I was passing through college, periodically poured instruction into that leaky receptacle sycophants refer to as my brains sometimes tells this tale to his class: 'I once had two pupils, two promising pupils, d'ye folla? and I took them into the College Park to teach them how to survey; one held one end of the chain and the other the other, one danced and the other sang, one was Charles Manners, the other was Percy French!'

One escapade at T.C.D. in the late 1870s inspired these verses.

After working for the Midland Railway French 'spent two years in Derry on my own.' One of his friends at Foyle and Trinity was John Ross, later to become Lord Chancellor of Ireland. Their collaboration continued with **The Mother-in-Law, Could Kilmainham Jail, and Doolin P.L.G.**

The most remarkable of my school-fellows at Foyle College was William Percy French. He surely had the makings of a great landscape painter. When a scene presented itself to his view, rich in varied colour, he became almost intoxicated at the sight. This feeling he had the power of communicating to others: I think he inspired in me a love of pictures and art. But artistic success was the last thing he thought about. His mission was to amuse the world in a way of his own, and he did it in a remarkable fashion. He delighted in composing and singing comic songs, accompanying himself on the banjo. To hear French render one of these songs with a perfectly solemn face was a thing one could never forget. I wrote several songs for him: one that he published has travelled far. It is called '**Andy McElroe**' – a private from the North of Ireland serving in the Soudan campaign.

(Sir John Ross, Lord Chancellor of Ireland)

My brother Andy said that for a soldier he would go,
So great excitement came upon the house of McElroe.
My father sold the bog-hole, to equip him for the war,
My mother sold the cushions of her Sunday jauntin'-car;
And when brave Andy reached the front, 'twas furious work he made;
They appointed him a private in the Crocodile Brigade.
The sound of Andy's battle-cry struck terror through the foe;
His foot was on the desert! and his name was McElroe!

Chorus: At least, that's what the letter said that came across the foam
To Andy's anxious relatives, awaiting him at home.
The papers say he ran away, whene'er he met the foe;
But that was quite unlike the style of Andy McElroe.

CHAPTER TWO:

CAVAN

The Garden of Eden has vanished they say,
But I know the lie of it still.
Just turn to the left at the bridge of Finea,
And stop when half-way to Cootehill.
'Tis there I will find it, I know sure enough,
When fortune has come to my call.
Oh, the grass it is green around Ballyjamesduff,
And the blue sky is over it all.

French moved to Cavan in March 1883, at the age of 28, living at 16 Farnham Street.

I had given up all hopes of work in Ireland and had packed my portmanteau for Manitoba, when I received a notice from the Board of Works that I was appointed Inspector of Loans to Tenants, and that Cavan was to be my headquarters. Three hundred pounds a year and travelling expenses was untold wealth to a bachelor boy with my simple wants, so having bought a new set of banjo strings and a tennis racquet, I set off to take up my duties. Luckily for me these duties required no expert knowledge whatsoever, and by 'layin' low and sayin' nuffin' I soon got an inkling of the business.

Reading his own work.

Going up a Cavan hill.

THE KINNYPOTTLE KOMICKS.

A varied entertainment, as before announced, was given by this amateur troupe of Christy minstrels; to a very large and appreciative audience, in the Protestant Hall here, last Friday evening. Pressure on our space prevents a detailed criticism of the performance—but we can say with truth, that all through it was a complete success. Musically, dramatically, and artistically, the troupe was well balanced, and very perfect in its way. Even the more difficult parts of Christy business were thoroughly well sustained; "Bones" and "Tambourine", achieving a veritable triumph; the "Lightning Limning" being quite a masterpiece. We can add with pleasure that the performance was free from the irreverence and indecency which sometimes detract from the merits of public entertainments. Accustomed as Cavan audiences have been to music of a high class, admirably performed; and fastidious as they in consequence have presumably become, we but re-echo a general opinion, when we say that nothing better of its kind has been presented to their approval than the entertainment of last Friday. The evening's amusement, so really enjoyed by all, reflects great credit on local energy and talent—energy and talent quite capable of commanding more than local success. It remains only to say that the object of the performance was the relief of the poor of Cavan; and we trust sincerely that [...] worthy may always have champions as [...] that the kindness of our [...] will pardon the expres- [...] may be " At [...]

EXCELSIOR

The shades of night had almost fled
As through a Cavan village sped
A youth who bore upon his tric-
Ycle this somewhat strange device -
            'Excelsior.'

The spokes were polished up, each one
Gleamed as it caught the rising sun,
And flashed with nickel-plated sheen
The axles of that strange machine -
            'Excelsior.'

'Don't be an ass,' the old man cried,
'The Cavan hills are hard to ride,
Take my advice and get a car.'
A voice responded from afar -
            'Excelsior.'

'Oh, stay', the maiden said, 'and rest.
Of course you know your business best,
But why you toil the live-long day -
I can't conceive, nor why you say -
            'Excelsior.'

'Fair maid,' the youth replied, 'I would
That I could stay with thee for good.
But ah, my worldly wealth is small,
And so I must obey the call -
            'Excelsior.'

'Begob,' twas thus the peasant spoke,
'But that's the quarest sort o' yoke.
I beg your pardon, sir, but might - '
A voice replied far up the height -
            'Excelsior.'

What motive urged his flying feet?
A rendezvous with maiden sweet?
- Alas, 'tis time that I reveal
The secret of thy triple wheel -
            'Excelsior.'

Methinks it was the greed of gain
Which urged him thus across the plain.
No rest thy wheels may know the while
They pay him eighteen pence per mile -
            'Excelsior.'

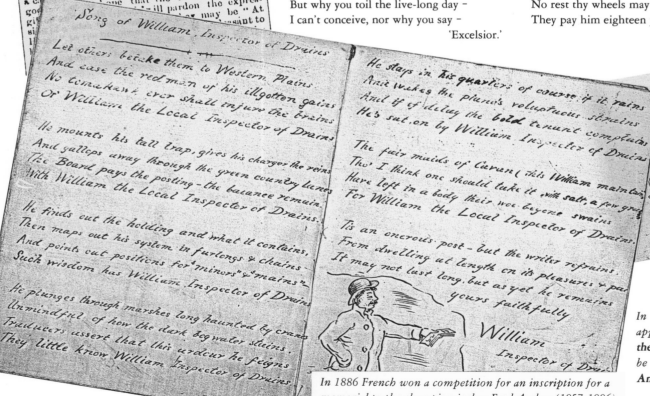

Song of William Inspector of Drains

Let others betake them to Western Plains
And ease the red man of his illgotten gains
No tomahawk ever shall injure the trains
Of William the Local Inspector of Drains

He mounts his tall trap, gives his charger the reins
And gallops away through the green country lanes
The Board pays the posting - the balance remains
With William the Local Inspector of Drains.

He finds out the holding and what it contains,
Then maps out his system in furlongs & chains
And points out positions for "miners" & "mains"
Such wisdom has William Inspector of Drains

He plunges through marshes long haunted by crane
Unmindful of how the dark bog water stains.
Traducers assert that this ardour he feigns
They little know William Inspector of Drains.

He stays in his quarters of course if it rains
Ance wishes the plund's voluptuous strains
And if it delay the bold tenant complains
He's sat on by William Inspector of Drains

The fair maids of Cavan (this William maintain
Tho' I think one should take it with salt, a few grai
Have left in a body their woe-begone swains
For William the Local Inspector of Drains.

'Tis an onerous post - but the writer refrains.
From dwelling at length on its pleasures & pai
It may not last long. but as yet he remains
      yours faithfully

    William
    Inspector of Drains

coming do...

In 1884 another song appeared, **The Cruise of the Canal Boat,** *later to be renamed* **The Mary Ann McHugh.**

In 1886 French won a competition for an inscription for a memorial to the champion jockey Fred Archer (1857-1886).

Here's to him who through life rode straight,
Straight as he rode for plate and for cup;
E'en Death's pale horse must have felt elate
As he sped through the Shadows with Archer up.

THE CAVAN WEEKLY NEWS, FRIDAY, MARCH 11, 1887.

Amateur dramatics.

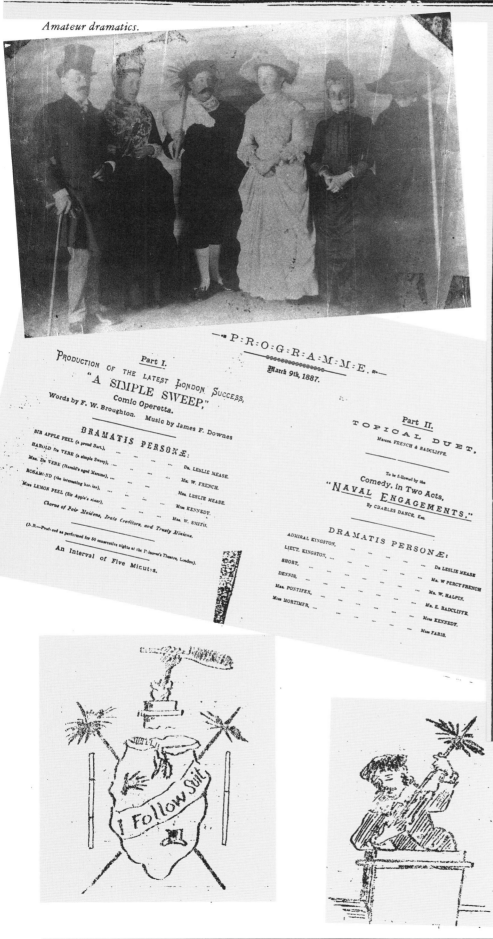

The opening chorus was well sustained by Messrs Radcliffe, Weekes, Jones, and Halpin, as the *Infuriated Creditors.* Then Mrs Mease in the solo, "I'm a Widow," called forth the plaudits of the listeners as the tones of her grand voice rose high and clear, filling the hall. Next followed a second chorus of *Creditors,* and then the *Sweep*—Mr. French—appeared. We have heard it said that his part in this piece is so suited to him that it might almost have been written for him. No higher compliment could be paid to his talent as an actor. And in the beautiful duet, "Our fate's indeed a sad one," sung by him and Mrs. Mease, his perfect ear, correct intonation, and careful study of the part, enabled him to do full justice to the exquisite music and to Mrs. Mease.

The chorus of maidens was filled by the Misses Clifford, Faris, Beatt, and Mathews, and was most effective and pleasing. The beautifully harmonised chorus, "Sighs may disguise a heart full of tears," being especially good.

But perhaps the gem of the piece was the charming duet, "Standing nigh my chamber lattice," sung by Miss Kennedy as *Fair Rosamond,* and Mr. French as the *Sweep,* which was rapturously *encored.* Miss Kennedy's fine soprano and her excellent acting gave much pleasure. We do not often hear such a voice; nor, off the stage, a finer appreciation of the situations to be developed, together with a knowledge of the technique of the drama not often possessed by an amateur.

Dr. Leslie Mease, as the proud Baronet, *Sir Apple Peel,* appeared late in the piece. His ability as an actor has long been recognised and that he did well what he undertook, goes without saying. But we think his *role* is comedy, and the limitations even of a comic opera are too severe for him. In the afterpiece he showed himself a real actor and to the manner born.

Mrs Smith as *Miss Lemon Peel,* sang sweetly, and the *Minions* in whom we recognised the gentlemen who represented the *Creditors* at the opening of the play, came on the stage near the conclusion, and their black masks, dark mantles and wonderful hats, formed a striking contrast to the light dresses of the maidens.

The *drop curtain scene* (from the brush of Mr W French) was a picture worth seeing—"worth alone, all the entrance money I paid for my family"—we heard one of the audience say. It represented a wall covered with advertisements and a bill poster at work regardless of that much contemned legend —*Post no Bills,* which appeared on a board above his head. There also appeared over the wall the familiar form of Head-Constable Lynch, an excellent portrait, with baton in hand; and the fixed and firm expression on his face that becomes a trusty servant of Her Majesty and a guardian of the peace. Beside him was the Town Sergeant whose appearance was quickly recognised, and as he had evidently given information to the *Head,* prompt arrest of the unfortunate "Corduroy" was imminent. As the later advertisements half-covered those posted sooner, the spectators read: "Mothers are you troubled in your rest by—Our water-proof boots worn by all the leading—Cockroaches killed by—The Cavan Militia! 1,000 men wanted to—Try our Infants' food—Stove Polish," and so on in an amusing jumble ending with: "Passages to Canada via—The Cavan Waterworks."

PROGRAMME.

March 9th, 1887.

Part I.

PRODUCTION OF THE LATEST LONDON SUCCESS,

"A SIMPLE SWEEP,"

Comic Operetta.

Words by F. W. Broughton. Music by James F. Downes

DRAMATIS PERSONÆ.

SIR APPLE PEEL (a proud Bart.),	Dr. LESLIE MEASE.
HAROLD De VERE (a simple Sweep),	Mr. W. FRENCH.
Mrs. De VERE (Harold's aged Mamma),	Mrs. LESLIE MEASE.
ROSAMOND (the interesting heroine),	Miss KENNEDY.
Miss LEMON PEEL (Sir Apple's sister),	Mrs. W. SMITH.

Chorus of Fair Maidens, Irate Creditors, and Trusty Minions.

(N.B.—Produced as performed for 50 consecutive nights at the Pinafore's Theatre, London).

An Interval of Five Minutes.

Part II.

TOPICAL DUET.

Messrs. FRENCH & RADCLIFFE.

To be followed by the

Comedy, in Two Acts,

"NAVAL ENGAGEMENTS."

By CHARLES DANCE, Esq.

DRAMATIS PERSONÆ:

ADMIRAL KINGSTON,	
LIEUT. KINGSTON,	
SHORT,	Dr. LESLIE MEASE
DENNIS,	Mr. W PERCY FRENCH
	Mr. W. HALPIN.
Mrs. PONTIFEX,	Mr. E. RADCLIFFE.
Miss MORTIMER,	Miss KENNEDY.
	Miss FARIS.

From **Fitzwilliam Square**, *sketches by Richard Orpen.*

THE TENNIS PLAYERS.

Then the noble Hee-haw-watha
Told them of another pastime,
Told them of the game of Tennis :—
How the young men and the maidens,
How the old men and the children,
Played at Tennis all the summer ;
How he tried to understand it,
Looking at them from a distance,
But he always failed to grasp it,
Though a Frenchman kindly told him
That the way the game commences
Was to try and strike the netting
With the first ball of the service ;
Then you get the next ball over,
Then you cry out, " Mine," or "leave it,"
And again you bang the netting,
Crying "hard luck," "hit the tape line,"
" Nuther inch an' I'd a' got it."
These, he told him, were expressions
He had heard among the players.

From 'White Lines, *a tennis tournament chronicle, Buxton,*
Text by French, sketches by Walter Pigot.

An' down from the mountains came the squadrons an' platoons,
Four-an'-twinty fightin' min, an' a couple o' sthout gossoons,
An' whin we marched behind the dhrum to patriotic tunes,
We felt that fame would gild the name o' Shlathery's Light Dhragoons.

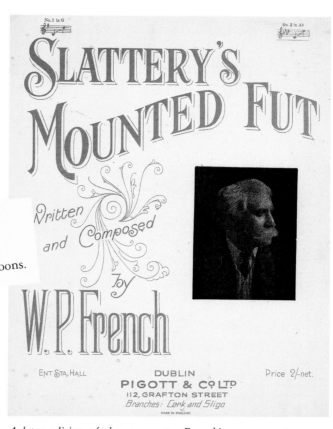

A later edition of the song copy. French's songs ran to many editions.

I was staying at Drominchin at the time, the Godley's home near Carrigallen. One evening the Rev. James Godley came in after one of his long walks, and told me how he had met the local flute-player and how he had paid his rent.

'I've paid up all me arrears, yer riverence,' said Phil the Fluter - for, as my readers have already surmised, 'twas himself that was in it.

'And how did you manage that?' said his reverence.

'I gave a ball,' said Phil.

'A ball!' cried his reverence. 'If my family asked me to give a ball I'd have to put my hand in my pocket - and I think I'd keep it there,' he added thoughtfully. 'Well,' said Phil, 'you'd make a hole in a couple o' pound given' *your* ball, for you'd have a young lady to play the pianna and cake and sandwidges an' other combustibles. Now when I give a ball I clear out me cabin, and lock up any food or drink in the cupboard. Then I put me hat behind the door, the neighbours come in bringin' their suppers wid them, and each putting a shillin' or two in the hat. I cock me leg over the dresser, throw me top lip over the flute and toother away like a hat-full o' larks and there they stay leppin' like hares till two in the mornin'!'

Then Phil the Fluter tipped a wink to little crooked Pat,
'I think it's nearly time,' sez he, 'for passin' round the hat.'
So Paddy passed the caubeen round, and looking mighty cute,
Sez, 'Ye've got to pay the piper when he toothers on the flute.'

French played 'a very nippy game of tennis, and had a low-cut shot that was not easy to return.' (J. W. Weekes) At a tennis party given by Dr. and Mrs. Mease, French met his future wife Ettie Armytage Moore. Her country home was Arnmore, just outside Cavan.

From **Racquety Rhymes,** verses by French, sketches by Richard Orpen.

Dismissal notice.

CHAPTER THREE:

DUBLIN

Live within my income?
Very much I doubt it;
What I'd like to know is
How to live without it.

Portrait by Connie Tyrrell-Lewis, Ettie's step-sister.

French was appointed editor of a new comic journal, **The Jarvey,** *at 49 Middle Abbey Street, Dublin.*

I had been sending humorous prose and verse to the *Irish Cyclist* for some time past, so when I called on the editor, R. J. Mecredy, and asked for a permanent post on the *I.C.* he told me he would do better than that, he would make me editor of a brand new weekly comic paper to be called *The Jarvey*. We started with no capital whatsoever, and the idea was to pay the artists and writers out of the profits of the first month. At the end of the first month there were no profits, at the end of the second month there were no writers or artists - except my very great friends, Dick Orpen and Eddy Radcliffe.

Sketch by Richard Orpen.

The Kerry Man and the Maid.

I have a song to sing, oh—
Sing me your song, oh—
'Tis sung to the ring of a well-strung string,
When the serve is swift and strong, oh,
'Tis the song of a Kerryman moping mum,
Who, from his distant home had come,
But saw no stroke, so his face was glum,
As he sat in the rear of a lady,
    Shady, shady,
    Miseree me, lackadaydee.
He heard men shout, " Well played, old man,"
But all the play that he could scan
    Was the back of the beautiful lady.

I have a song to sing, oh—
Sing me your song, oh—
'Tis sung to an air that has made men swear,
That they wished girls at Hong Kong, oh ;
'Tis the song of merry maid peerly proud,
Whose hat was high, and who laughed aloud,
At the groans of the Kerryman moping mum,
Who, from his distant home had come,
But saw no stroke, so sat quite glum,
    At the back of a beautiful lady,
        Shady, shady,
    Miseree me, lackadaydee.
She heard them say, " Umbrellas down,"
But then the sun would burn her brown
    And that wouldn't do for the lady.

I have a song to sing, oh—
Sing me your song, oh—
'Tis sung to the crash of " a Renshaw smash,"
And it tells of a righted wrong, oh,
'Tis the song of a ball from a champion bat,
That broke the brolly, and bashed the hat,
And cannoned on to the dude who sat
    By the side of the beautiful lady,
        Haydee, haydee,
    Miseree me, lackadaydee.
And the Kerryman said, " If I had the chance,
Upon the brolly, I'd like to dance
    And the hat of the beautiful lady."

'Drifted into literature and arts' was how French later described this period.

CAVAN CHEZ LUI.
BY WILL WAGTALE.

The town of Cavan is situated on the fragrant banks of the river Kinnypottle. The widest part of this river is the smell, which in some places extends for miles.

Cavan is celebrated for its fair women and brave men. The former are so numerous and so beautiful that a complete list of them would never give anything like the number. The men are not so beautiful, but they are very brave. One of the bravest is Major Lindsay (he is probably Colonel Lindsay by this time). There is a legend extant that he fought and vanquished Jem Mace, the eminent pugilist ; some say the battle was drawn, others that it was " overdrawn," but as Jem has never alluded to the combat, it looks as if he was ashamed of having been defeated.

There are several banks in Cavan, but as I never had anything to put into them, and none of them let you overdraw your account, I can't tell much about them.

Mr. Thompson, of the Bank of Ireland, is a great sportsman. He started early last 12th of July or 20th of August (I'm no sportsman, so I don't know the exact date), armed to the teeth, and after blazing away for some time, he rose half a brace of beater.

Mr. Thompson fired, but only succeeded in wounding the animal, who fell into the middle of a lake, and as Mr. T. had shot his dog early in the day, he was obliged to return empty-handed.

This is the story as I heard it, and as it would take " Weekes " to disprove it, I let it stand.

Mr. Norton, of the " Ulster," is chiefly noteworthy for not being notorious.

All the bank managers are married men, especially Mr. Boyd, of the Provincial. At present he is more girled than Boyed, as most of the family are of the female persuasion.

There are several solicitors in Cavan. In order of height, they are Messrs. R. Allen, W. Halpin, H. P. Kennedy, and S. Jones.

They are, all four, splendid men in the full bloom of their youth and beauty, always eager to help others, and to help themselves afterwards ; ever ready with advice, and are all flourishing like green baize trees.

(The fact is I have no money to throw away in libel actions, or I'd have a slap at every man-jack of them.)

Cavan has two great educational centres — The Jail and the Royal School. They are closed at present ; the attendance having fallen off considerably of late years at both of these seats of learning.

Strangers visiting Cavan are usually pointed out the house in which the Editor of THE JARVEY once resided. The landlord is Charles Stuart, a lineal descendant of Prince Charlie's. His enemies say this is all pretence. This, however, would seem to prove some connection with the Pretender.

The Cavan branch of the House of Stuart is a lodging house. " Sic transit gloria Monday."

Cavan is a fairly healthy place, though there are four doctors there.

Will Wagtale was a French nom-de-plume.

French, now aged 36, married Ettie Armytage Moore on 28th June 1890 at St. Stephen's Church, Dublin. Their honeymoon was spent at Castle Howard, Avoca.

The marriage of Mr. Wm. Percy French, second son of Christopher French, J.P., D.L., of Clonyquin, county Roscommon, and Ethel Kathleen, youngest daughter of Mrs. Armytage Moore, and the late Wm. Armytage Moore, of Arnmore, Cavan, took place at St. Stephen's Church, Dublin, on June 28th. The wedding party was confined to the immediate relations of the bride and bridegroom, in consequence of the illness of the Dowager Countess Annesley, aunt of the bride, from whose residence it had been previously arranged the wedding should take place. Mr. and Mrs. French left for Castle Howard, the residence of Colonel Howard Brooke, lent to them for the occasion.

EDITING THE JARVEY

I had married on the strength of my income as editor, and a happier and more hopeful couple cannot be imagined. I knew nothing about the business and was often three or four columns short in the 'make up.' The criticism on our first number by Jakes McCarthy of the *Freeman's Journal* is worth recording. 'We have before us the first number of a journal devoted to art and humour. Some of the jokes we've seen before – some we haven't seen yet.'

Ettie, at the time of their marriage. The newly-weds lived at Victoria Lodge, 3 St. John's Road, Sandymount. 'How extraordinarily happy they were, just like two children, laughing all the time,' noted Mrs. Houston, the rector's wife.

Sketch by Ettie.

There was a young man who said "Why
Do you ride with your saddle so high?"
Said his friend, with a smile,
"I do it for style,
Though it's painful, I will not deny."

UP GOES THE PRICE!

On a chair in an office a little Wagtale
   Sang. "We'll owe the wheel oh, the wheel oh."
And I said to him "Willie Wag, why do you wail,
   Singing 'We'll owe the wheel oh, the wheel oh.'
Is your cash in a bank that is likely to break,
Or is it some villainous pun you would make";
But still he replied with a mournful shake,
   'Oh, we'll owe the wheel oh, the wheel oh.'

"I intended to purchase a bike," he began,
   "(Sing 'We'll owe the wheel oh, the wheel oh'),
And pay in instalments—an excellent plan.
   (Sing 'We'll owe the wheel oh, the wheel oh.')
But now a new bike I'm unable to buy,
Though to save up my salary weekly I try,
And though Alec responds to my mournful cry
   Of 'We'll owe the wheel oh, the wheel oh.'

For *The Cyclist* the sad information supplies
   (Sing 'We'll owe the wheel oh, the wheel oh'),
That the price of materials steadily rise.
   (Sing 'We'll owe the wheel oh, the wheel oh.')
There's coal and there's iron gone up so high,
That steel is found dreadfully dear to supply,
And a discount no longer we get when we buy,
So 'We'll owe the wheel oh, the wheel oh.'"

—:o:—

TO THE EDITOR OF THE IRISH CYCLIST AND ATHLETE.

Sir,—I enclose a short poem, which I hope you will think up to the standard of your Stanley Show number.—Yours faithfully,

HENRY W. LONGFELLOW.

Comes a marvellous invention
  From the workshops of Belfast;
At the famous tyre's dimension
  All the makers gaze aghast.

Pity and contempt are blended
  In George Hillier's lofty stare;
Ah, he has not comprehended
  What it is to ride on air.

Is vibration but a bogey?
  Is it but an empty dream,
Dreamt by some enfeebled fogey
  Drifting down life's sombre stream.

We ourselves have felt the jingle,
  Felt it in each hand and limb;
Felt the jolt and jarring mingle,
  Till the very eyes grew dim.

Now the Antelope and Raleigh
  Glide along the stony street,
Referees and Pilots dally
  With the obstacles they meet.

And men cry in exultation,
  "Here is what we all require;
Here's the death-blow of vibration,
  Death by the 'Pneumatic' Tyre."

Songs from this year also included **Ben Bolt.**

The allotted life of a Dublin comic journal being two years, I was not altogether surprised when R. J. told me the Xmas number of 1891 would be our last. That expiring effort was a great one. I advertised that the number would consist of new and original stories and poems by all the great authors from Chaucer to Conan Doyle, and then set to work to write them myself!

French had a particular facility for parodying the work of other authors. (Source material: Burns' To a Mouse, *Wordsworth's* We Are Seven, *Kipling's* A Song of the White Man, *Longfellow's* A Psalm of Life, *Swinburne's* Autumn in Cornwall, *Browning's* My Last Duchess.*) These examples are not, in fact, from that final edition of* The Jarvey, *but a selection from the many hundreds of parodies that French wrote throughout his life.*

JACK SPRATT COULD EAT NO FAT (Done into Lowland Scotch by Rabbie Burns)

Ye ken the tale o' guid man Sprat,
Wha couldna eat a bit o' fat,
But then his wife made up for that,
So 'twas nae matter.

What she could eat Jock wouldna hae
And sae the vittles passed away,
The dog and cat the neighbours say
Found empty platter.

LITTLE BO-PEEP
(Wordsworth's version)

I walked with her upon the hill,
Her grief was very deep,
Her tears were running like a rill,
For she had lost her sheep.

'What were they like, my gentle maid,
Were they some special kind?'
'They all had heads in front,' she said,
'And all had tails behind!'

'Their bodies were between the two,
Their mouths were full of teeth,
And - this, perhaps, may prove a clue -
Their legs were underneath.'

'If they have legs,' I cried with joy,
'Your tears you may refrain,
For 'tis their legs they will employ
To bring them home again!'

BAA BAA BLACK SHEEP
(A la Rudyard Kipling)

(And this is the song of the black sheep,
And the song of the white sheep too,
And the awk and the armadillo
And the crocodile knows its true.)

'Have I wool?' said the Baa Baa Black Sheep.
'You ask me have I wool?
When I yield each year
To the shepherd's shear
As much as three bags full.'

'Have I wool?' said the Baa Baa Black Sheep.
'Go forth to the frozen zone,
And my wool they wear
Where the polar bear
And the walrus reign alone.'

'Have I wool?' said the Baa Baa Black Sheep.
'Examine the sailor's socks,
Retaining their heat
Through the driving sleet,
And the gales of the Equinox.'

(And this is the song of the Black Sheep,
And the song of the white sheep too,
And they make up this song
As they wander along
And it's not very hard to do.)

LITTLE BOY BLUE
(By Henry Wadsworth Longfellow)

Tell me not in mournful numbers
That the cow is in the corn,
If it is Boy Blue that slumbers
Let him wake and blow his horn.

If the cow has left the shadow
Of the tree where it had lain,
If the sheep is in the meadow,
Let the echoes wake again.

Cows are real - cows are earnest,
If he does not chase her now,
He will find ere eve returnest
All the corn is in the cow!

GOOSEY GOOSEY GANDER
(Swinburne's version)

Oh whither, oh why, and oh wherefore
Great goose thou art gosling no more,
With none to caress thee nor care for,
Wilt wander from floor to floor?

Is it upstairs thy Gandership's goal is,
Or dost thou descend from above?
To where in her Holy of Holies
Low lieth my love.

Where I met with the man who is hairless
And holding his left leg in thrall,
Propelled him, all pallid and prayerless,
From attic to hall.

TAFFY WAS A WELSHMAN
(Re-told by Robert Browning)

That is the bolster, I have hung it where
You others hang some trophy from the war
Over the mantel - 'tis an old story - Care
To hear the details of it? - Right you are.

This Taffy was a Welshman and a thief -
The terms are not synonymous, my friend -
He may by now have turned a newer leaf,
How runs the saw 'Tis ne'er too late to mend.

The man was hungry, starving - had no food,
He knew that I had much to eat and drink
And so he came and stole - you know the mood,
The act needs no analysis, I think.

Then mark the sequel - Taffy stole my beef
And I, who hold the law's delays in dread
Ceteris paribus stalked my Cymric thief
And stole the bolster from beneath his head.

He never woke - ah, there's the master hand -
To rob a larder that is not so hard.
If you should ever want some robb'ry planned
And executed - there, Sir - that's my card.

THE OLD CURIOSITY SHOP

I became personally acquainted with the well-known Percy French shortly after he had opened 'The Old Curiosity Shop' at No. 31 Little Denmark Street, Dublin. I can still recollect seeing him in his new Trilby hat, dark coat and grey trousers, standing leisurely within the doorway, hands behind his back, while chatting with a charming vision in a dainty coloured frock – slim, divinely fair, but with that faintly pink complexion indicative of an early call to the Eternal Land of the Ever Young. The predominant feature of the 'Old Curiosity Shop' was pictures – engravings, sketches, paintings in oils and in water-colours. My own secret attraction was nothing more than the feathered headgear of a Red Indian chieftain, which was on a ledge behind Percy's easel. French showed me an Arab scimitar, a Hindu dagger, a Zulu shield, and a shabby old tricorne hat, which he said 'might have belonged to Sarsfield – or maybe to Dick Turpin.'

(J. W. Hammond)

His first musical comedy and first collaboration with Houston Collisson. The title was later changed to **The Irish Girl.**

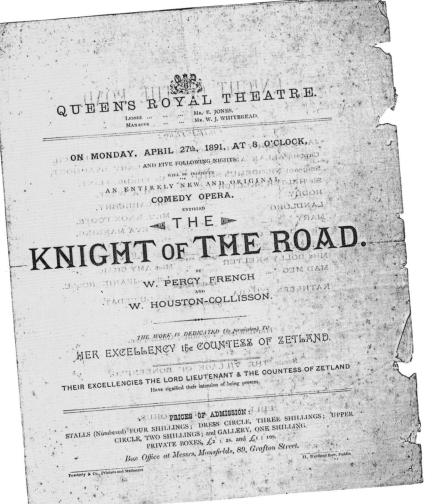

Poster by Ettie.

The Jarvey having gone down with colours flying, I had to find another source of income as soon as possible, for I had married 'The Ray of Sunshine' and the greatest event in a woman's life was only a few months ahead. However, I turned to musical comedy and found it there. Have you ever tried to write a musical comedy? What fun it is – for you, I mean – not for the audience.

It was William Houston Collisson, Mus. Doc., who first asked me to write him a libretto, and suggested an Irish setting for our joint effort. I had just been reading an old book entitled *Irish Rogues and Rapparees* and the career of Jack Freeny the Wicklow highwayman struck me as a subject for dramatic treatment. His pressing the clean-cut end of a cabbage stalk against the forehead of a young officer on a dark night, and telling him that he would blow his head off if he made a sound, showed that he had a sense of humour; so I told the little doctor I had my hero ready made.

> So the gentlemen pulled out their purses of gold,
> And handed them over to Freeny the bold,
> Says Freeny, 'Me boys, ye got off mighty well,
> I'd have fleeced ye far more *had I kept a hotel.*'

In 1891 a well known name became inseparably linked with mine, the name of Percy French – author, poet, humourist, painter, engineer, mathematician, entertainer and best of men. No living man has got such a grasp on real Irish humour. When Percy French sends me a new MS, on a postcard or on part of a band-box, to set to music as a song, it usually means that I have to sit down and rock with laughter at the real fun contained in it before I dare think of setting it to music. His humour is never forced, but always subtle.

(Houston Collisson)

The Dublin papers took us up and boomed us as the first composer and writer who had produced a real Irish Musical Comedy, and we had packed houses every time. Musically I think it is the best thing the doctor has ever done; and my up-to-date libretto equals any – but the report that my Trumpeter is dead proves to be false, so I say no more.

French's wife Ettie, his Ray of Sunshine.

MR. W. PERCY FRENCH AS "JACK FREENY," 2ND ACT.

WHEN I WAS A CHILD

When I was a child I was meek and mild
And quite as good as gold;
I was, in fact, in word and act
A pattern to behold.
My father would stand with a stick in his hand
My morning hymn to hear,
If I missed a line he would fan my spine,
While mother enlarged my ear.

They brought me up on the strictest plan –
That's why I became a highwayman.

Chorus
They brought him up on the strictest plan –
That's why he became a highwayman.

Oh, Sunday was gay, all my toys put away
And a book put in my hand,
Called 'Faith and Work' by Ignatius Burke,
Which I never could understand.
Then Tommy McGee would whisper to me,
'Let's go off and fish for perch'.
I'd have loved to go but I answered 'No',
As I passed on my way to church.

They brought me up on the strictest plan –
That's why I became a highwayman.

Then as a rule my life at school
I couldn't quite enjoy,
For I was licked by the boys and kicked
For being a model boy.
On the last pretex' I'd have wrung their necks,
I was strong for a boy of my size;
But I knew I'd be whaled by my dad if I failed
To bring home the good conduct prize.

They brought me up on the strictest plan –
That's why I became a highwayman.

I got so good, men said I would
Be dead before my prime,
So my parents thought they really ought
To choose my profession in time.
I was going to say that I'd like some day
To run away to sea,
Or else enlist, but my father said 'Whisht,
He was made for the Ministree'.

They brought me up on the strictest plan –
That's why I became a highwayman.

SOME SAY THAT TO FLOAT

Some say that to float
Down a stream in a boat
Will bring any man to your feet:
And some people talk
Of a moonlight walk
As an equally certain receipt.
But better than dreaming on silvery stream,
And better than moonlight or star,
Is just to contrive to go for a drive
On an Irish jaunting car.

Oh! the Irish jaunting car!
From Bantry to Ballinagar –
You always begin
By tucking her in
On the side of the jaunting car.
On an Irish jaunting car,
If fond of the girl you are,
It takes a good while
To fix her in style
On the side of the jaunting car.

When you fly round a turn
One thing you must learn
That really you ought to know,
Put your arm round and grip
Her, for fear she should slip –
And don't be too quick letting go.
For when your arm's placed
Round her elegant waist
There might come a terrible jolt –
If your arm wasn't there,
She'd be kill'd, I declare,
So there's reason for holding your holt.

Oh! the Irish jaunting car!
When it comes to a jolt or a jar,
You have every right
To be holding her tight
On the Irish jaunting car.
When out on an outside car
The weather is really no bar,
If it comes on to rain
You never complain
On the Irish jaunting car.

There's a flush on her cheek,
And you venture to speak
Of making her some day your own:
Her eyes are quite kind,
But she begs to remind
You 'that really, we are not alone.'
Oh, the driver is blind,
And the horse doesn't mind
If you're going a bit too far,
And the crack of the whip
Covers lip meeting lip
On the back of the jaunting car.

Oh! the Irish jaunting car!
Your fortune 'twill make or mar:
For you're woo'd and you're won
Before you have done
On the Irish jaunting car.
On the Irish jaunting car
You may trust she's your lucky star,
For Cupid has set
His cunningest net
On an Irish jaunting car.

On 5 June 1891 a daughter was born, Ethel Florence Cecilia, but tragically both mother and daughter died: Ettie of septicaemia on 29 June at home, aged twenty, and the baby on 5th July at Cloonyquin. Ettie is buried in Mount Jerome Cemetery, Dublin, and the baby in the grounds of Elphin Cathedral, not far from Cloonyquin.

PARADISE

Somewhere east of the Euphrates,
Hidden now from human eyes,
Men tell me that the gate is
Of an earthly Paradise.

Some scorn the ancient story –
Vague tales of long ago,
But I have seen the glory –
I have been there – and I know.

I have found it – I have found it,
Though now 'tis but a dream,
I know the woods that bound it,
I know the silver stream.

• • • • •

Sweet thoughts we two were thinking
As we wandered hand in hand,
And as the sun was sinking,
We found Enchanted Land.

She turned to me and kissed me,
With the Love Light in her eyes,
Oh wealth and fame have missed me,
But I've been in Paradise!

Not east of the Euphrates,
Nor guarded from above,
Ah no! the Golden Gate is
Where Love has answered Love.

And high-born hearts and lowly,
May find these fields and know
The song serene and holy,
Our hearts heard long ago.

The shades of night were falling,
Even then across her way,
She heard the Angels calling,
She wept but might not stay.

So when the shadows hide me,
And darkness veils mine eyes,
Sweet Spirit, come and guide me,
Once more to Paradise.

ONLY GOOD-NIGHT

Only 'good-night' sweetheart,
And not farewell,
Though for all time thou art
Where Angels dwell.

Though for a time those eyes
Lose their soft light,
Let there be no good-byes,
Only good-night.

Though for a time they toll
Thy passing bell,
'Tis but good-night, sweet soul,
And not farewell.

O'er thy sweet lips I sigh –
Lips cold and white,
There! – that is not good-bye,
Only 'good-night'.

L'ENVOI

Only the seabird now its way may wing
From crested wave to crest,
And great cloud galleons in the azure swing.
'After life's battle,' they are murmuring,
'There shall be rest.'

The long-lost glories of life's fairyland
More nearly gleam,
And joys that years ago two lovers planned
Seem to the watcher on that lonely strand
Not all a dream.

NOT LOST BUT GONE BEFORE

Once, only once, upon a time,
We heard the bells of faerie chime,
And through the golden nights and days
They sang their Elfin roundelays.
The world and we were in our prime
Once, only once, upon a time.

Has Fairyland for ever flown?
- The darkness falls on me alone,
For on my sweet companion's eyes
There shines the light of Paradise.
The heights of joy I cannot climb
As we did once upon a time.

Oh, loved one of the far away,
I know that we shall meet some day,
And once again walk hand in hand
Through all the realms of Fairyland.
And Heaven's own harps around us chime,
As they did - once upon a time!

After his wife's death, French disappeared into the country for a while, later moving to The Mall, Strand Road, Baldoyle. This door, with the panels painted in oils by French, comes from that house.

More songs appeared.

My recital of 'Song, Story and Sketch' originated when Dick Orpen and I went to hear a lantern lecture by Harry Furniss on the London Parliament. During the interval Orpen suggested that I should write a lecture on Dublin, and that he would illustrate it with caricatures of celebrities in and out of society. In a month we appeared in the Antient Concert Rooms with a lantern lecture entitled *'Dublin Up-to-Date.'* I remember I began 'Ladies and gentlemen, there are two sides to everything - except Harcourt Street Station.' What a small joke - but Heavens! what a laugh! It taught me the value of topical allusions. Orpen's pictures got round after round of applause, and during the interval he and his young brother 'Billy' drew lightning sketches in coloured chalks. *'Dublin-Up-to-Date'* went on tour, and as Dick Orpen, being a rising architect, could not come with me, I devised a comic landscape in coloured chalks which I gave as an interlude.

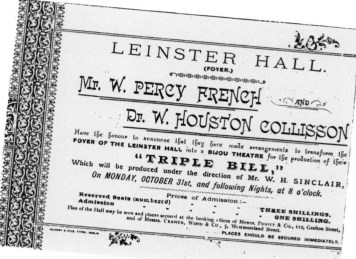

His second musical comedy was
Strongbow, *in which he played the part of a harper.*

ENTERTAINMENT BY MR. PERCY FRENCH.

Last evening, in the Molesworth Hall, Mr Percy French gave an entertainment under the title of "Dublin up to Date" and "Social Absurdities." There was a fairly large attendance. The entertainment comprised selections from Mr French's most successful sketches and songs. It was illustrated by limelight sketches of a humorous character, and Mr French also accompanied himself on the banjo in his numerous comic songs. In "Social Absurdities" Mr French kept the audience in continual merriment by his clever lampooning of certain extremes in modern social life. He dealt with the modern bazaar in general and with many of its interesting features, and touched off all with a light and pleasing humour. He next gave a "few words on art," which were also happily conceived. The next feature of the entertainment was an amusing account of certain experiences of the "Rev. Peter Binks" in his effort to teach a lady to ride the bicycle, and his sufferings at a children's party. In the "Dublin up to Date" section of the entertainment the most attractive feature was the "photographic album," in which many well-known figures in the life of Dublin were humorously presented in characteristic positions. Mr French's vocal contributions included "Mulligan's Masquerade," "The young couple on the stairs," and a "Serenade arranged for a Baritone and a Bull Dog." A capital evening's entertainment was enjoyed by all.

PURDON'S IRISH FARM

IRISH STEW

It's an island in the ocean, p'r'aps you knew,
It is always in commotion, it is true,
For each petty king's ambitious
To have everything he wishes,
And so a frequent dish is Irish Stew.

Oh, our energy's surprising over there,
And the soil we're fertilizing everywhere,
Till the fruit hangs down in tassels,
'Tis on grapes we feed our vassals,
And we're building lots of castles in the air.

We have cattle there I tell you - never fear,
And salmon we could sell you when it's dear,
In the dark we may be gropin,'
But we're mighty good at hopin,'
And the market will be open say next year.

We have whiskey that's illegal, now and then,
We have poultry from an eagle to a hen,
We are strong at emigration,
But we've whips of education,
And we'll be a thriving nation dear knows when.

AN "UP-TO-DATE" INTERVIEW.

No. XXXI.—Mr. W. Percy French.

"Strongbow" a Great Success.

Hints About His Next Move.

[SPECIAL TO THE "EVENING TELEGRAPH."]

IT goes without saying that to write even a moderately successful book of words for a comic opera is a task which requires both originality and wit. Just at present these productions are more or less the rage in Dublin, and it is reported that there are several in the stage of incubation. Dr Collisson and Mr. French, however, were the first to take the field, but long before Mr. French's name was associated with "The Knight of the Road" he was widely known as a writer of humorous songs, and of clever lawn tennis skits, which were much appreciated by the patrons of the Fitzwilliam-square tournaments. Mr. French

is a graduate of Trinity College, and by profession a civil engineer, but if there are few persons who can write as clever a song, he says himself "that there are many able to construct a better bridge." Naturally one of the first questions I asked him was whether "Strongbow" was drawing good houses?

Very good indeed, was the reply, so much so that we have

DETERMINED TO RUN IT ANOTHER WEEK.

The author is of the opinion that it is much the best thing he has written, and he spoke in high terms of the manner in which it has been staged by Mr. Whitbread, who, he added, hopes to see it soon placed in one of the London theatres. This gave me an opening to remark that some of the Dublin papers seemed to think that the subject of the opera had not been happily chosen. I suppose, I said, that you have seen the statement that it is founded on an event in Irish history which should not be lightly treated of.

Mr. French—I have, but I don't think I can very well argue the point. My reply to such criticism is simply that it never occurred either to Dr Collisson or myself that exception could possibly be taken to it on that ground. I confess I have little reverence in my composition. I see the humorous side of things too plainly.

May I ask you write to the music, or was the music written to your words?

Mr. French—The words of the comic songs were written first. The words of the situations gave the composer the situations, and he told me how many songs he wanted, where they should come in, and who should sing them. The opera was

WRITTEN AT SIX WEEKS' NOTICE,

which was the principal reason that I had to obtain Mr. Brindley's assistance. I may mention that as he has a very sensitive ear for metre, he did not relish having to write to an air, for instance, which required two words in the first line, seven in the second, four in the third, and so on.

If it is a fair question to ask was the "Knight of the Road" a financial success?

Mr. French—I am glad to say it was, and when reproduced during the horse show week we invariably played to full houses. I was left entirely free as to the choice of a subject, but was bound to lay the scene in Ireland, and to introduce a regiment of Highlanders.

Your "Dublin up to Date" proved a very decided hit; how did the idea of giving the entertainment originate?

Mr. French—Attending one of Harry Furniss's lectures illustrated with caricatures, it struck me that with Mr. Orpen's assistance I could do something to amuse the Dublin people. We gave our entertainment at the Castle, and his Excellency was so much pleased with Mr. Orpen's lightning sketch in water colours that he expressed a wish to purchase it. The artist did not care to dispose of his work, but requested the Lord Lieutenant to accept it, which he did.

It was stated that you were going to do the provinces—has that scheme fallen through?

Mr French—The production of "Strongbow" interfered with it, but in any case I have not as yet been able to arrange with regard to a business manager, and I regret to say I am very

IGNORANT ON COMMERCIAL MATTERS

myself—Almost as ignorant as I am of politics, but my want of knowledge on the last named subject I think rather an advantage than otherwise.

Which of your songs have you found the most successful?

Mr French—"Slattery's Mounted Fut" was purchased by Messrs Pigott. "Abdallah-Bulbul-Ameer" has had the largest circulation, but this brought small gain to me, as it was pirated by a London house, and I have twice seen it illustrated in London papers without any name being attached. The last war song in "Dublin up to Date" is going very well.

With regard to pirating, of course you have legal redress?

Mr. French—Undoubtedly, but this involves expense and other difficulties, and as I before mentioned I am not a good business man.

The general experience of persons who live by the pen is that literature is not a very lucrative calling—perhaps you have been more fortunate?

Mr. French—Well, I have made writing pay, and am at last able to let other irons cool. It is now some years since I made out a long list of all my friends and sent them post-cards to say a work of mine was on sale at all the booksellers. They replied asking for a gratis copy, and saying they would tell their friends! What they told their friends I don't know; but none of them bought the booklet.

You edited the Jarvey I think for some time?

Mr French—Yes for two years which is about the usual duration of the life of an Irish comic paper. It started, however, with many things against it. The name was not a good one, and we had barriers of prejudice to break down, which, though we won many friends, we did not succeed in doing before our exchequer gave way. I greatly fear that London and New York have absorbed our best humorous talent, and am certain that a paper to pay now-a-days must be full of personalities—a sort of writing I take no interest in. Another reason that

A DUBLIN COMIC PAPER SEEMS DOOMED TO FAIL

is that it is impossible to get it properly pushed. Local shopkeepers much prefer inducing their customers to buy a London publication.

Before leaving Mr. French I had an opportunity of inspecting some water-colours which decorate the walls of his study, and are his own work. A piece of moorland scenery by him is exhibited at present in the Hibernian Academy.

Asked whether he had much literary work in hand? he replied that he and Mr. Orpen would probably have another illustrated lecture ready for the autumn, and that Dr Collisson was anxious that he should settle on a subject for a new opera as soon as possible. "As a matter of fact," he said, "I am reading up the 'Spanish Armada,' 'Brian Boru,' 'The Battle of Benburb,' and several other historical episodes which might be likely to lend themselves to my purpose."

Considering that it would be interesting to get Mr. French's opinion on the relative merits of the entertainments given by Messrs Grossmith and Furniss respectively, I asked him to tell me briefly what he thought of those artistes. Grossmith he considers wonderfully finished, and his piano playing marvellous; but he pointed out that his songs read badly, and if given by anybody else would probably fall flat enough. With the greatest admiration for Furniss as a draughtsman, he sees no reason to admire him as a humorous lecturer, nor to refrain from expressing in strong language his contempt for the bad taste which he exhibited in his letters on Dublin society. This is an old matter now, but it will be considerably older before it is forgotten. Mr. French further informed me that his taste for writing showed itself at a very early age, and, during school vacations in conjunction with Mr. Alfred Godley, who has since distinguished himself greatly at Oxford, he brought out a manuscript magazine for private circulation. It seems a pity that the Tercentenary Committee did not entrust the preparation of the College farce jointly to Mr. French and Mr. Edwin Hamilton, instead of placing it in the hands of men who have still to win their spurs. The last named gentleman (lately interviewed for the Evening Telegraph) is to write a prologue, but Mr. French appears to have been overlooked. No doubt, however, if he cared to announce a lecture on "College up to date" he would secure a large attendance at the Antient Concert Rooms on some night during that week. We conclude with a couple of Mr. French's ditties—

MEDICAL ETIQUETTE.

Sir Diagnosis Stethoscope Parietal De Brown
Was perhaps the most astute of all the medicos in town,
And through all his course of study
And his practice he would let
No sentiment divert him
From his code of etiquette.

One day when in the hospital,
A case he chanced to see
Being treated for "insomnia"
By Max Hillary, M.D.,
He saw that Max was treating it
Most ignorantly, yet
He couldn't interfere—you know
It wasn't etiquette.

He vowed the patient could not live
Beneath that upas tree.
'Twas thus that he referred to
Old Max Hillary, M.D.,
His fingers fairly itched to try
His " Hypodermic Jet,"
But couldn't well suggest it,
As it wasn't etiquette.

The days rolled on, the case grew worse,
De Brown would shake his head ;
He never proffered his advice,
But murmured, " As I said ;"
And when the patient died, he went,
With feelings of regret,
And dropped a tear upon the bier—
But this was etiquette.

Lines by Our Own Old Fogy.

'Twas in the prime of summer time,
An evening calm, but cool,
When two or three young College lads
Went forth to play at pool,
And I, my son, went with them—why?
Because I was a fool.

The billiard rooms were not too swell,
The marker's name was Pat.
My only game is bagatelle
(I'm not too good at that),
And yet I needs must play at pool ;
My son, I was a flat.

Of course, we called for S. and B's,
Of course, I drank my share,
We thought it manly, if you please ;
O, Lord—it makes me swear—
To think, in passing nights like these,
What lunatics we were.

Then some one gave me a cigar ;
I lit it at the gas.
Before I'd smoked it very far
I turned as green as grass ;
For why ? I ne'er had smoked before—
My son, I was an ass.

Oh ! wasted nights ; oh ! vanished years ;
Oh ! gin, cigars, and pool ;
List ! list ! my son, with all your ears,
Or else hereafter you'll,
Perchance, revile yourself like me,
As ass ! dolt ! idiot ! fool !

*French was beginning to make a
living as an entertainer.*

IN A BIJOU THEATRE.

'A Triple Bill at the Leinster Hall—
"Little Lord Faulty Boy," "Midsummer Madness," and a Sketch
by Mr. French.

When the curtain went up Miss Rose was
discovered in the capacious embraces of a
garden chair, trilling a simple lay. Hardly
had she reached the middle of the second line
when she discovered that her maiden medita-
tions had been intruded upon by a humorous
curate. The curate, armed with a practi-
cable tripod, no sooner mounted upon a practi-
cable tripod, no sooner discovered his error
than he was thrown into a very humorous
confusion. Recovering himself with considerable difficulty he begged to be informed
what place it was into which he had thus un-
conscionably thrust himself.

"This," replied Miss Rose, with some as-
perity—for though fair of form her temper
was tart—"this is a private lunatic asylum,
and you will doubtless find yourself quite at
home here!"

The humorous curate no doubt deserved
this unkind remark, for it is an unpardonable
thing to thrust yourself into a lady's company,
disturbing the hallowed peace of a serene
siesta. Being a humorous curate, however,
the Rev Peter Film received the well-worn
witticism with much seriousness, and, under
the mistaken impression that he had really
strayed into a retreat for disordered minds,
allowed himself to be drawn into a series of
entanglements at once embarrassing to himself and amusing to the beholder. For instance,
when Lady Betty, whom he understands to be
an "inmate," introduces herself in a whim as
Mrs Langtry, he, to be equal to the occasion,
presents himself as Bishop Peter, of Rumtifoo.
To humour the lady he allows her pay unmis-
takable attentions to him until he incurs the
suspicion of the family butler. Grogson hears
mysterious references to a certain "plate,"
this being, of course, a photographic negative.
Grogson jumps to the conclusion that the alleged
bishop has his eye on the spoons. The Rev
Peter has photographed the Lady Betty, who
is considerably disturbed by the discovery that
...pears on the ground-glass in the camera
...which a popular fallacy ascribes
...Antipodes. The...

MR. W. PERCY FRENCH'S FORTH-
COMING VISIT TO KILKENNY.

Mr. W. Percy French will visit Kilkenny on
Tuesday, 5th inst., in his humorous musical
and polyphonic entertainment, entitled
"Laughing Gas." Mr. French will give selections from his sketches, banjo, songs, etc., and
we feel sure his engagement in Kilkenny will be
a successful one. The comic illustrations will
be displayed by a powerful oxy-hydrogen
lantern. Mr. French has always been a great
favourite with Kilkenny audiences. His performances are ever amusing and never vulgar, and
are appreciated by the most critical gathering.
The Press of all shades of opinion, both in the
metropolis and the provinces, are unanimous in
their expressions of approval of the entertainment.

MR. W. PERCY FRENCH'S ENTER-
TAINMENT.

Athlone is shortly promised a visit from
"Du Val's successor" or "The Irish Grossmith" as Mr W Percy French has been
variously named. He is advertised to appear
at the Barracks Theatre on December 1st.
He will sing all his newest songs and give
several new sketches, and is to be accompanied
by the charming lady harpist, Miss Miriam
Bernard, who, with Mr W J Cookson, clarionet
soloist, also of London, has been spending the
past summer in a series of engagements in
this country. Miss Bernard is also a soprano
vocalist, and sings to her own accompaniment
on the harp. Such a programme speaks for
itself, and should certainly be well supported
in Athlone.

Fact of the matter a man doesn't...
To see himself just as he is,
But to see somebody very much...
And with a presentable phiz...
The art of retouching has caus...
And portraits no longer ann...
For even in my face they sho...
And your's is for ever a joy...

They obliterate the foot...
And they smooth...
wrinkle.
And they turn a fog...
To a wonderfully you...
And though she is a...
For the camera the...
For we never, neve...
In the portraits of th...

The kodak, I mention...
gratitude,
For in the hands o...
It takes you in some n...
Causing you endle...
Perhaps you are tryin...
To keep off a chil...
And you find that so...
detective,
Has fixed you t...

And you find yo...
Or you find yo...
With someth...
way,
Reclining on your sn...
It takes you with a rail...
Or endeavouring to...
coffee,
Or struggling with st...
They press a little bu...

Dr Collisson's music...
is, perhaps, not intende...
Its lack of originality...
its cleverness, and it i...
catchy.
Mr French contri...
of "Midsummer M...
Faulty Boy," a von...
culties and dange...
sketching tour.
...know what it...
genuinely amu...
"Little Lo...
Triple Bill...
sketch, and a...
with themse...
will, doubtl...
was the I...
the char...
Mr H T...

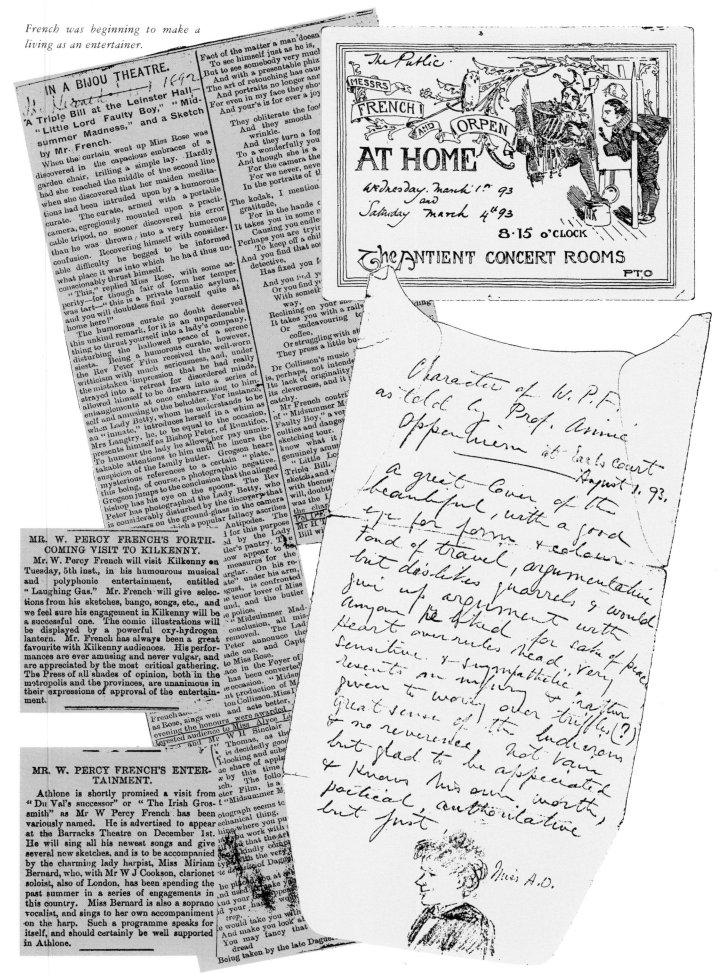

Character of W. P. F.
as told by Prof. Anima
Oppenheim at Earls court
August 1. 93.

A great lover of the
beautiful, with a good
eye for form & colour.
Fond of travel, argumentative
but dislikes quarrels, & would
give up argument with
anyone he liked for sake of peace.
Heart over-rules head. Very
sensitive & sympathetic. Inattentive.
Resents an injury & neither...
given to worry over trifles (?)
Great sense of the ludicrous
& no reverence. Not vain
but glad to be appreciated
& knows his own worth.
Practical, authoritative,
but just.

Miss A.O.

From the **Tyrone Constitution.**

and Hobart £12—all Pneumatic
MACFARLANE & Co, Omagh.   80-

ENTERTAINMENT IN THE GRAND JURY ROOMS BY MR. W. PERCY FRENCH.

On Friday evening, 6th inst., an entertainment of a highly humorous, musical and artistic character was given in the Grand Jury Rooms, Omagh, by Mr. W. Percy French, and those who had the good fortune to be present enjoyed a couple of hours genuine amusement. The attendance, notwithstanding the fact that another meeting was being held in town at the same time, was fairly good, and had, at least, the advantage of being most appreciative and select. Appreciative, as evidenced by the frequent and hearty applause which greeted the performance, and select on account of the charge for admission being slightly above the average. A number of people who would have felt inclined to purchase a two-... ticket, hesitated doing so owing to those ... reserved; while some persons who ... to spend one shilling were doubt-... remained away. We think the ... charges of two shillings and one shilling, ... of three, two and one, would have ... matters considerably and ensured a ... house. The holding of another meeting at ... same time must certainly be deplored, and ... responsible for fixing the date can hardly ... any reasonable excuse, considering that Mr. ...'s entertainment was advertised for fully ... weeks prior to his arrival. The exercise of a ... consideration and forethought on the part of ... committees would easily prevent two important meetings occurring on the same night; ... nothing could possibly be lost, but on the contrary, something gained had the meeting been ... postponed, or held on a different date. And ... furthermore, when our town is visited by a distinguished stranger, we think it would be only ... right and proper to extend to him, if not a welcome ... at least a certain amount of courtesy. ... The programme consisted of three parts, light, ... and colour. In part I. Mr. French commenced by informing his audience of the difficulties ... in choosing a profession—how he ... experienced ... thought of becoming a doctor, a lawyer, a clergyman, a soldier, but finally abandoned those ... and took to playing the banjo and ... his own composition, was admirably ... ... being war songs. One of the songs, which is ... , and is entitled "Soldiers three." The ... of the song are full of clever humour, and ... chorus is given by the author is irresistibly ... and runs as follows:—

We don't want to hear the cannons rattle in
    the battle,
We don't want to hear the bullets roar any
    more;
We'll gather in the gory field of battle,
    the cruel war is o'er.

... notions and engineering a failure—were ... with in a humorous and delightful style, ... which he sang with banjo accompaniment, ... music of the Mississippi shore, which was ... with much applause. "Our local penny ... at which the rector of the parish is ... to take the chair, came in for ... share of attention; the chairman's ... being especially good, as well as the songs ... recitations as rendered on those occasions. ... representations of the village choir—the forgetful ... some local talent, &c., &c., gave evidence ... superior ability, and evoked hearty plaudits; ... particularly the guitar song of Miss Julia Golightly, a lady of uncertain age, who sings in an uncertain voice, "Oh, where are the dees of my childhood?" also Mr. Peter M'Quillan's rendering of "Lord Ullin's datter." All the items encored, and "The ..." concluded the first part of the programme, and received loud applause, being very ably represented by Mr. French.

During the short interval which followed the audience enjoyed a rare musical treat in listening to the piano playing of Dr. Collison. The pieces ... was one of Mendelssohn's compositions, and needless to say it was brilliantly executed. Later on he again appeared, and gave some musical selections composed by himself; Mr. French previously explaining that for these he would not be responsible. This performance was loudly applauded and encored, Dr. Collison bowing his acknowledgments.

Part II. was devoted to shade, or "Some sidelights of Irish life," and the comic illustrations were shown by a powerful oxyhydrogen lantern, which was manipulated by Mr. R. C. Orpen in a very creditable manner. How we impress the Saxon—his previous ideas—Punch's Irishman were all cleverly portrayed, and as each ludicrous character or picture appeared on the screen the audience could not refrain from indulging in a hearty outburst of laughter. "The night that Miss Cooney eloped" was sung in excellent style as the various characters represented appeared in rapid succes-

...AGH, FRIDAY, APRIL 1

...tion on the screen. On hearing of the elopement Miss Cooney's parents and brother are terribly ...flicted, chiefly because that young lady eloped with a sweep, they vow vengeance against ... sweep and threaten him (in his absence) with ... sorts of dreadful things, until he suddenly appears on the scene and shows a determination to fight when they immediately change sides, and receive him with open arms. The key-note to Hibernia asking the way—a stroll through Dublin were ... markably good items. Much amusement ... caused by the appearance on the screen of "a ... clerk" and the description given of him by ... French. He is seated on the office-stool enjoying his luncheon and chatting with a fellow-clerk. When a stranger comes in to cash a cheque, ... takes the cheque, examines it furtively, while continuing the conversation with his neighbour, ... than suddenly confronting the stranger, as ... pushes the cheque towards him, says—" Put your name on the back of that." This was followed several really good things, viz.:—How we ...—how we entertain—the police force—the slums the street singer—the suburbs, and to ... acquainted with the habits and accent of ... Dublin people and the southerns these representations, so truly and cleverly given by Mr. French must have been thoroughly enjoyable. The singing of that very popular song of Mr. French's, "Mrs. Hannigan's aunt," together with the comic illustrations, created roars of laughter, as also did a serenade—the couple on the stairs—a duet for a tenor and a cat which concluded the second part of the programme.

Part III consisted of the painting of a large water colour drawing by Mr. French during which the following subjects were humorously introduced and touched upon:—Try art—In Topsy-Turvey land —The customs of the Country. An unfriendly critic, where to sketch and what—Killarney. Its aboriginal inhabitants. The Colleen Bawn—The oldest inhabitant—The School Children "What's he paintin'? I dunno." The drawing was painted upside down with a blunt shaving brush, and occupied only a few minutes. On Mr. French holding it up to the audience, they instantly recognised its merit and the artistic taste which had been displayed, and greeted the unique performance with long and hearty applause. The entertainment was concluded with the singing of "God Save the Queen." Mr. Collison playing the accompaniment. As a fitting conclusion to this report, and in order to give an idea of the musical ability and poetic genius possessed by Mr. French, we append some pretty and touching lines written by him and recently published in "The Social Review."

"Only the old, old story,
    But changing my world for me;
The hills have a halo of glory,
    There's a song from the distant sea.

Only a whisper merely,
    A voice in the twilight dim,
But it whispered he loved me dearly,
    And wondered if I loved him.

And tho', in the ages olden,
    The story has often been told,
To melt has brought more golden
    Thoughts than the heart can hold.

GYPSOLINE, the new Sanitary W...

In the chorus of Strongbow was a 23-year-old from Burmington
House in Warwickshire, Helen Sheldon. She had been at school
with Alice Lindé, the young Dublin singer also in the cast. Helen,
known as Lennie, married French, now aged 39, on 24th January.
She was aged 25, the daughter of John and May Sheldon. This
Dawson Street studio was their first home.

THE marriage of Mr. W. Percy French to Miss Helen Sheldon, of Burmington House, Warwickshire, took place on the 24th of January, a
Burmington Church. The officiating clergymen were the Rev J. Wheeler,
Vicar of Cleobury, Mortimer ; and the Rev. R. Espinasse, Vicar of Burmington. The bride was married in her travelling dress—a pale grey,
trimmed with buttercup silk and beaver, and large hat to match. The
three bridesmaids—Miss Baird, Miss Shaw, and Miss Whittle, cousins
and niece of the bride—wore cream ; and Master Geoffrey Whittle brown
velvet with cream silk vest. Mr. Alfred Godley, Dean of Magdalen
College, Oxford, acted as best man. The numerous presents were displayed at the reception after the ceremony, and at four o'clock the happy
pair left for London *en route* for Ireland.

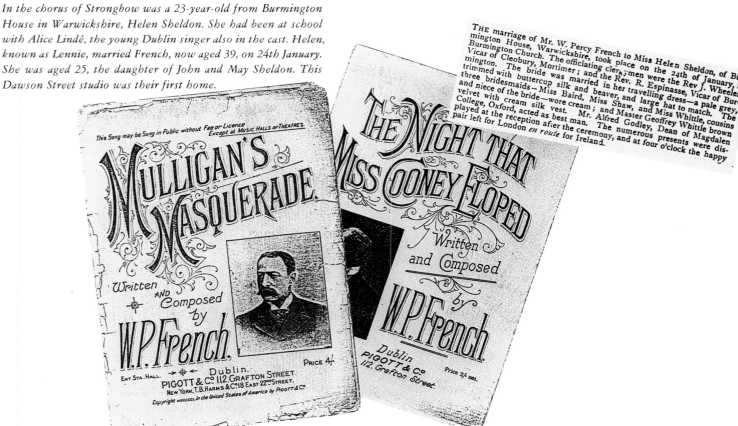

The Frenches moved to 35 Mespil Road. 'We are living by the canal: do drop in.' On 4th November 1894 a daughter was born, Ettie Gwendoline.

Pencil sketch of Lennie by Walter Osborne, made during one of the sketching club meetings that French organised.

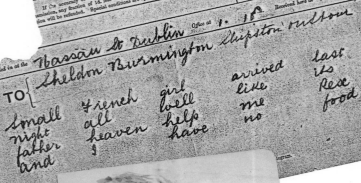

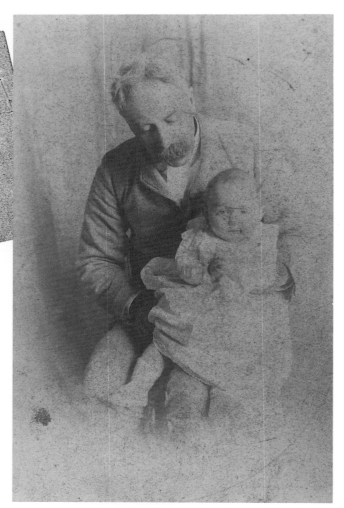

'My White Haired Laddie', by Lennie.

With baby Ettie. In the painting of Cloonyquin House on p.1 she is in the pram under the tree.

Mr. W. Percy French's "Höhezeit," which took place last Thursday night in the Antient Concert Rooms, fully justified its title by giving a "high time" to a large and fashionable audience. Our "most practical joker" (as Mr. Edwin Hamilton dubbed Mr. French some time ago) appeared in several new and original sketches. He commenced the programme by appearing with a flag of truce, to shield him while he read telegrams—apologies for non-appearance—from Rothschild, who was waiting for a penny night; Path, who was unable to perform "Home, Sweet Home," and a step-dance to banjo accompaniment; and other celebrities. Mr. French's lectures on "The Art Career of Johnny Jones" and "Unnatural History," both illustrated with great cleverness and lightning rapidity by Mr. Orpen, caused a great deal of amusement. Miss Alyce Lindé both sang and looked charmingly, as she always does; and Mr. Allen's banjo, guitar, and mandolin band were delightful in their instrumental performances, and much pleased the audience by singing and accompanying Mr. Harry West's song, "Honey O!" Mr. Walter Pigott and Mr. Carroll were enthusiastically recalled for their nigger song and dance. A couple of very unusual items were supplied by Mr. Martin on the copophone (musical glasses), on which he is able to play most beautiful chords; and by a countryman from the South, who gave two songs in the native language, to the great delight and amusement of the audience. Mr. North was in excellent voice, and sang most sweetly, both in his solo and duet with Miss Lindé. Dr. Collisson conducted, but, being obliged to leave before the end of the concert, the final accompaniments were played by Mr. Craig. Mr. French has every reason to be pleased with his benefit concert, for not only was there a large crowd inside the room, but a small one outside, which was unable to gain admittance. * * * *

'I suppose you've not been to Drumcolliher?
Ye haven't? Well now I declare,
You must wait till you've been to Drumcolliher
And see the fine place we have there,
There's only one street in Drumcolliher,
But then 'tis a glory to see;
Ye may talk till you're dumb, but give me ould Drum,
For Drum is the place for me.'

MR. W. PERCY FRENCH'S ENTERTAINMENT.

Mr French's repetition of his new entertainment proved very successful last evening at the Antient Concert Rooms. He commenced by giving a short account of some travels in Irish rural districts, of which he saw much last summer, and gave graphic descriptions of adventures on railways and at hotels. A sketch of a drama performed by a travelling company in a small country town greatly delighted his audience, and afforded him opportunity to sing the praises of 'Drumcollogher, down by the borders of Clare,' a new song, which ought to become popular, as both words and air are very good. The latter part of the entertainment included a new collection of society sketches of the kind by which Mr French first became so well known. The Rev Peter Binks' account of a children's party he had just attended, with incidental remarks on children in general, was delightful, and his sufferings during the games of 'Burning house,' and 'Mad buffalo,' emulated those of the 'Private Secretary.' The instrumental part of the programme was carried out very well by Miss Pauline Burke, who played as one of her pianoforte solos a charming 'Swing song' of her own composition, and Mr Martin, whose copophone playing was charming.

MR. W. PERCY FRENCH'S ENTERTAINMENT.

Yesterday Mr. W. P. French gave the first matinee of his new musical sketch to a large and fashionable audience, and we shall not be surprised if he has to repeat it many times during the holidays. A performance of this kind sets one wondering whether the establishment of an entertainment of the "German Reed" type would not be a success in Dublin, where theatres and music halls are few, and there is a certain section of the public who attend neither. Of Mr. French's new songs there are three which ought to "stay," for the sake of both words and airs—"Drumcollagher," "Mulligan's Masquerade," and the "Killyran Wrackers." Mr. French gave the first, and last, with short "sketches" attached to them, and convinced his audience that not only his matter is as good, but his manner even better than ever. He was assisted by a clever pianist in Miss Pauline Burke, and by Mr. J. M. Martin, who is coming deservedly into notice with his charming playing on the musical glasses. To-night there will be an evening performance of the same programme.

Songs from this year also included **The Killyran Wrackers.**

The Grey Wolf Wave of Dawn

On 13th March a second daughter was born, Mollie Helen.

COME-ALL-YE

Oh! a sailor courted a farmer's daughter,
Who lived contagious to the Isle of Man.
With warbling melodies he did besought her
To marry him before she'd marry any other sort of a kind of a man.

But the farmer's daughter had great possessions,
A silver teapot and two pounds in gold;
And says she 'Would ye marry me, me bould salt water sea-sailor,
If I threw them into the ocean cold?'

'Oh,' says he, 'I'd marry you, me heart's enchantment,
If you had nothing but your father's curse!'
So she made up a bundle of all her grand possessions
And threw them into the water . . . that ends that verse.

But the sailor he could swim like a duckling,
So into the water he dived down deep below,
Got hold of the bundle and swam away chuckling,
To think of the times he'd be having when he landed down in Ballinasloe.

But the farmer's daughter was kilt with the laughing,
To think of the bundle she'd made up out of a stone . . .
Oh! a sailor courted a farmer's daughter,
But now he's wishing that he'd left the girl alone.

His collaboration with John Ross continued, in another topical song,
The County Council.

THE CHILDREN'S PARTY
or
THE STORY OF THE LION THAT
WOULDN'T EAT PARSLEY

(Peter Binks enters with hair slightly dishevelled, and a worried and depressed expression.)

I have just come back from a children's party. I am one of the survivors. There are not many of us.

When I got to the house the servant asked me to leave my clothes in the hall. Of course I did not do so, but I am sorry now that I didn't - they were my best clothes; now they're not clothes at all - just garments for the poor. I went into the room, and they gave me a cup of tea - the small child crawling between my legs got the cup of tea, the one climbing up the back of my chair got the saucer.

Then we fed them for a solid hour; after that one would think that they would have liked to lie down for a bit, but they didn't; we played round games then. Have you ever played a game called 'Burning House?' The children were a fire brigade - *I* was the burning house. I find you needn't confine yourself to throwing water at a burning house; you can throw cushions or books or fire-irons.

Then we played 'Mad Buffalo;' the children were a pack of wolves - I was the mad buffalo. I'm glad I wasn't born a mad buffalo, it has a weary life. Most of its time is spent under the sofa avoiding wolves . . . Then they said 'Let's play *Dragging the Pond!*' I came out from under the sofa and said, 'No, children, we won't play *Dragging the Pond* '(I knew who was going to be the pond), 'But I'll tell you a story instead.' I thought it would keep them quiet, and I didn't know how hard it is to tell stories to small children. You see, they interrupt you so, and ask so many questions, and want all the particulars.

(With one foot on a chair, and as if surrounded by children on the floor.)

Now, children, you sit down there, and I'll tell you the story. Just there - oh! anywhere. Yes, UNDER the carpet if you like - stop biting my leg!

(Sits on back of chair with feet on the seat.)

No, it's not more comfortable up here, but it's safer. Yes, away from the wolves . . .

Well, there was once an old woman - no the old woman wouldn't eat you - yes, a lion would EAT you - oh! yes, there's a lion in the story - yes, a tiger's worse - yes, a lion's worse than a tiger; well, HE said it first dear, he said it FIRST.

Well, the old woman lived in a wood. No, there were no lions in the wood. Oh! the next wood was full of lions - yes, and tigers too, bulging out of the tops of the trees - they couldn't come down on account of the lions.

Well, the old woman had a son called Jack, and - NO! Jack wouldn't eat you - I wish he would - yes, we're coming to the lion now -

The old woman sent Jack down to water the garden . . . What? . . . Oh, the usual sort of garden. Roses and spinach and polyanthuses, and - yes, there was lots of parsley in the garden.

No, a lion wouldn't eat parsley; he'd eat Jack without it - glad to get him.

So Jack went down to the well -

NO! THERE WERE NO TIGERS IN THE SPINACH! Yes, but a blackbird isn't a tiger! Besides spinach is green and a tiger is yellow; the gardener would have noticed a tiger if there'd been one - Yes, he was a very careful man - a Scot - yes, he had two rakes, one for slugs, and one for tigers. So Jack went down to the well - yes, we're coming to the lion - yes, the lion's in the well! When Jack came down, there was a GREAT BIG LION sitting in the well - yes, on the water . . . I SAID he was on the water, and he WAS on the water! . . . I don't care! Lions DON'T sink! . . . They have some way - yes, they waggle their tails underneath. They tread water with their tails.

And Jack ran to his mother, and said 'There's a great big lion sitting in the well!' And she said 'You silly boy, that's not a lion, it's your Uncle Thomas'. So Jack went back to the well, but he found that it wasn't Uncle Thomas, but it WAS a great big lion; and it jumped out of the well, and gobbled him up.

The Moral? . . . Oh! the moral is that if you believe all your mother tells you, you'll be eaten by a great big lion.

On 10th August in the previous summer French arrived late for an entertainment he was due to give at Kilkee, County Clare, owing to a series of incidents on the narrow gauge West Clare Railway. French subsequently took the railway company to court for loss of earnings.

From the **Clare Journal.**

ANOTHER ACTION AGAINST THE WEST CLARE RAILWAY COMPANY—AN HOUR WITH PERCY FRENCH "FREE OF CHARGE."

The succeeding case was also one in which the West Clare Railway Company figured at the defendant side of the court, the "man with a grievance" in this case being the well-known society entertainer, Mr W. Percy French, who in his effort to fasten due liability on the company for his failure through their break-down "en route" to enable him to turn up in time at an advertised performance at Kilkee, which damage, he estimated at £10, provided an hour's entertainment for the court free of charge."

Mr H C Cullinan, instructed by Mr J Cullinan, C.S., appeared for Mr French.

Mr Murphy again represented the Company, instructed by Mr Healy.

Mr French it would seem from Mr Cullinan's opening statement had advertised a concert on the 10th August last at Kilkee. He dared say his Honor had heard of Mr French, a gentleman of family and position who had been obliged to supplement his income by giving variety entertainments in different parts of the country. He advertised this entertainment at Kilkee, the doors to be open at 7.30 and to commence at 8 o'clock. He left the Broadstone terminus at 7.40 that morning expecting to arrive at Kilkee at 3.25, going by that route although it was 12s more expensive that the other one, to get there. He made the connexion at Ennis, but when he got to Miltown Malbay the train did not proceed any further. It was eventually 8.20 when he arrived at his hall, when he found his audience had dispered. They had waited until past 8 o'clock. He did give an entertainment but there was a very sparse audience.

His Honor—Did'nt he get then all he was expecting?

Mr Cullinan—No, sir. Persons came there and went away and did not pay Mr French, but his old accompanist will be able to tell that his monies for the night should be £14 while he only sues here for £10.

Mr Murphy—Very moderate.

Mr Cullinan said there was another thing. Mr French had a magic lantern also, but it did not arrive at the Hall until 9 o'clock, when it was too late to be put up. Mr French was injured in his professional reputation as well. Having regard to Mr French's position he should say there was a very graceless defence on the part of the company and it reflected very little credit on whoever was responsible for it.

Mr Healy—You will have to restrain counsel, sir (a laugh).

Mr Murphy said their first defence was that the company were not responsible inasmuch as it was an inevitable accident. Of course, if his Honor ruled against them, their only defence would be to measure the amount of damages.

Mr French then ascended the table and gave the history of his eventful experience on this fatal day. Leaving Broadstone at 7.40 a.m., he had got near Miltown-Malbay, on the "narrow gauge" system, when his troubles began. Here the train slowed down and finally it came to a stop at the station at Miltown-Malbay, where they were detained for three hours. He was aware that an engine had been telephoned for to Ennis, and it duly arrived, but notwithstanding, they were kept for some time on the siding.

His Honor—I suppose they were waiting for some other train? Yes, your Honor. The train from Kilkee came and passed, and then I thought we would go on, but we waited for the train from Ennis.

His Honor—Why were you left there? I can't tell, that's for the company to tell you. They did not explain why they waited for the train from Ennis. When I got to Kilkee the doors were not open. There were about 30 people outside the hall. There were about 30s booked in the hall. I let them in and gave an entertainment.

His Honor—If you had time to advertise it it would have been larger, and besides it was damaging to your professional reputation. You had no time to decorate the hall?

Mr French—No. Mr Enright, who had my magic lantern, arrived about 9 o'clock, when it was too late to put it up. Mr O'Callaghan, my accompanist, was in Kilkee before me. It was injurious to my reputation—it was not up to my usual standard, and besides there was a breach of contract with the audience.

By Mr Murphy—Plaintiff said the entertainment was to be held in Moore's Concert Hall, which would hold about 350 people. He gave one there before by himself and he got £14 in the house. With the assistance he had he should say he would have got more now. Mr Enright was a favourite singer. He should take about 100 two shilling tickets and the balance in shillings. He had sent a telegram to the proprietor that the train was late. It was advertised to begin at 8 o'clock, and it was 8.25 when he began.

Have you any reason to think that the Hall would be full there that night? It was the height of the season there.

His Honor said it should be full, unless the people were entirely drinking whiskey there, and that was he was told what they did, and the more public houses they get there, the more they want. It was impossible to give them enough of them. Here was this gentleman coming down to try to improve them and give them a taste for rational amusement and the railway company resist his paltry claim of £10. He did not know who directed them to do it, but he would distinctly say that unless they proved they were not responsible for the accident he would decree them. But of course it was the Almighty they would blame, and his Honor here told a humourous little anecdote of his own experiences on one occasion when crossing the Channel from France when there was an explosion on board, which one of the crew attributed to "le bon Dieu." In his experience of the West Clare railway they did not mind what he said—they go on appealing against his decisions, but the people who hear the appeals did not know as much about the company as he did (a laugh).

Mr Murphy—It is right to take every advantage (a laugh).

His Honor said he did not think it was. He knew a good deal about by companies in England, and they made it a rule to go to law as little as possible.

Mr Murphy then began his cross-examination of Mr French, who had shown himself as much at home in the witness box as he is on the stage. He said he had entertainments in Ennis.

His Honor here observed that rather than submit to such an ordeal he would decline ever coming down here again and let them drink their whiskey (a laugh).

Mr French said he had taken £8 to £9 at the Ennis Town Hall.

Mr Murphy—And Ennis is a fairly good place, of 5,000 inhabitants.

Mr French—But it is not a watering place in the season.

his apt retort caused no little amusement in court which was increased to a regular peal of laughter when his honor gave his view that Kilkee was a watering place where very little water was consumed in the season.

Mr Harvey—Except in mixtures, sir. They are afraid of the animalculae, and they reduce the water (more laughter).

Mr Murphy asked how many people did Mr French have in the Ennis Hall.

Mr French estimated a couple of hundred, but he could not at the same time see what had this to do with the present case.

His Honor—It does not make much impression on me, but let him go on.

Mr O'Brien, Clerk of the Peace—The Land Commissioners wont listen to the value of the next adjoining farm (laughter).

This finished Mr French's evidence, and it must be admitted he was an excellent witness.

Mr. Ed. O'Callaghan was the next witness and he said he thought £10 a very moderate sum to claim.

Mr Murphy said he would admit Mr O'Callaghan's audience.

His Honor said he did not blame Mr Murphy at all for his defence, he only blamed the gentlemen who instructed him. It was a shame to come forward and resist so moderate a demand. It was a scandalous proceeding on the part of the company.

In reply to Mr Murphy, the witness said there was a crowd of about 30 out side the house. He had been speaking to half a dozen who told him they would have gone but for the delay.

His Honor said Mr French would lose in reputation by such a thing.

Mr Cullinan—The next time he would not have one at all there.

For the defence, Mr George Hopkins, locomotive superintendent on the system, was examined to show that the accident was one that could not be avoided. At Lahinch he said the engine driver found that one of the injectors was working badly, and on getting to Miltown he found the water supply going down, and it was getting dangerous to proceed. It was necessary to draw the fire.

The engine was in perfect order when starting, and got out of order on the road? Certainly. We had a similar case recently.

His Honor asked the witness could he swear the engine was in order when starting, and he replied certainly. It was one of their newest engines, the Lisdoonvarna. Weeds had got into the boiler and choked it.

Witness explained how this might happen at the time of taking water. He saw the weeds himself taken from it.

Asked by counsel why the train waited so long at Miltown-Malbay, witness said perhaps the idea was to get the two trainon by the one engine.

His Honor said that was exactly his idea.

To Mr Murphy—These engines are all washed out once a week. He had nothing to say to the traffic arrangements.

Mr Sullivan, Manager of the System, said that on this date he had a telephone from Miltown to send out an engine, as the 12.40 one was unable to go on as the injector had got stuck. He at once telephoned to Kilkee to bring on an engine to bring the passengers there. He wrote to Mr French apologising for the accident and saying of course it was inevitable.

His Honor said the point was his keeping the train on the siding when he had an engine to bring it on, until the train from Ennis came.

His Honor here asked Mr French how long had he been kept on the siding after the train from Kilkee had gone to Ennis.

Mr French said about half an hour. He got into the train that came on from Ennis, but his luggage was all kept back for the other train as they said there was no time to change.

Mr Sullivan—We did everything we possibly could to get over the difficulty. If the driver went on in the condition the engine was, it might be a serious thing.

His Honor—That's quite right.

Mr Sullivan—When I telephoned the engine came from the other section. It came from Kilrush.

His Honor—You contradict Mr French; he says it came from Ennis.

Mr Sullivan—I will prove it came from Kilrush.

His Honor—The railway company ought really take more care than they do about these accidents. Do these accidents occur often?

Mr Sullivan—No, sir.

His Honor—Are you sure there was not one lately to a train coming in?

Mr Sullivan—There might be a break-down.

His Honor—Does'nt it break down every second day? (laughter).

Mr Sullivan—Oh, no, sir.

His Honor—They tell me so in Kilrush.

Mr Sullivan—They are telling you lies, sir.

This closed the evidence and his Honor said he should give a decree for £10 and expenses.

ACTION AGAINST THE WEST CLARE RAILWAY COMPANY.

This was an appeal brought by the West Clare Railway Company, from a decision of the County Court Judge, giving a decree for £10, in an action at the suit of Mr Percy French, the well known entertainer, for loss and damage sustained by reason of respondent having been delayed whilst travelling on the line to Kilkee.

Mr Redmond Barry, B.L. and Mr Murphy, B.L, instructed by Mr W. Healy, solr, appeared for the appellants.

Mr H. C. Cullinan, B.L. instructed by Mr J. Cullinan, C.S, appeared for the plaintiff.

The plaintiff deposed that on the 10th day of August last he had advertised a variety entertainment at Kilkee, to commence at 8 p.m o'clock He arrived in Ennis from Dublin the same day, and left by the 12 30 train for Kilkee. The train was timed to arrive at Kilkee at 3.30 p m. The train slowed up coming into Miltown Malbay, and pulled up altogether when it came into the station. He was compelled to remain there for five hours before he could proceed on his journey and when he arrived at Kilkee it was 8.30, o'clock. His luggage did not arrive until 9 o'clock, and consequently he could only give a part of the entertainment. When he arrived at the Concert Hall, Kilkee, he found the receipts were only £3, a large number of people having gone away for want of someone to open the doors in his absence. He had given performances in Kilkee before this occasion, and often realised £14 in a single night.

His Lordship asked what was the nature of the entertainment.

Plaintiff—The title of the entertainment was "Society Sketches."

His Lordship—It took in all objects?

Plaintiff—Very suitable for seaside resorts.

His Lordship—And no doubt the society were in Kilkee?

Cross-examined by Mr Barry—"Our Railways" was one of the items on the programme for that night (a laugh).

Plaintiff here remarked he had written a song on the West Clare railway in consequence of the mishap, and repeated a few lines as follows:—

> If you want to get to Kilkee
> You must go there by the sea,
> And not by the wild West Clare.

(laughter). He meant to have the song sung at the next entertainment.

His Lordship—Do you mean to tell me you were so impressed by the incident that you wrote a song about it?

Plaintiff—Well, I was not impressed at the time (a laugh).

Cross-examination continued—He would probably have taken a car from Miltown, but he was told an engine was coming on to take them to Kilkee.

His Lordship said plaintiff was not bound to take a car. He had agreed to travel by the railway.

Plaintiff continued—I telephoned to my agent in Kilkee about the accident to the train, and told him I was going on.

His Lordship—You have read in Pickwick where he represents the trials on the stage?

Plaintiff—I have, my lord.

His Lordship—Well, when you go back to give your next entertainment take care you don't represent this trial (laughter).

Mr George Hopkins, Locomotive Engineer, West Clare Railway, deposed that the engine attached to the train on the day in question was the best engine the company had. The driver of the train on the day in question found when he reached Lahinch that the water in the boiler was giving out and he was compelled to put up at Miltown-Malbay. He attributed the accident to some weeds having got into the injectors when the boiler was being filled with water.

Further evidence having been heard,

His Lordship said he would look into the law, and reserved his decision.

Lough Swilly *(County Donegal)*

SONGS AND SHADOWS.

PART I.

THROUGH ERIN'S ISLE:
DRUMCOLLIHER—
THE SPORTING FARMER—
"HOW WE BEAT THE FAVORITE"
(WITH A STICK).
PATSY'S HARE AND OTHER WILD
ANIMALS.

"OUR MUSICAL REVIVAL."
SHORT BUT THRILLING DRAMA:
"THE MAID AND THE MINIONS."
FINANCIAL RELATIONS.
AND A BALLAD OF THE WAR.

I MEET A THEATRICAL MANAGER—
HIS NEW VENTURE.
BOUNDER'S
"BEVY OF BEAUTEOUS BLOOMERS,"
THEIR SONGS—
"HANG THOSE 'OLD FOLKS AT HOME.'"

PART II.

OFF THE TRACK—
BUNRUSH BY THE SEA—
OUR BAZAAR—
THE CAFE CHANTANT !
A SCOTTISH CYCLE AGENT OBLIGES—
MAGUIRE'S BICYCLE.
THE YOUNG LADY RECITER—
THE COMIC SINGER—
THE PRIDE OF PETRAVORE
McBREEN'S HEIFER.

THE PETTY SESSIONS COURT—
A CROSS SUMMONS

EARLY IRISH ART
"THE MANIKIN, THE MASHER, THE
MAID AND HER MOTHER."
THE ASTONISHINGLY RAPID DEVELOP-
MENT OF A YOUNG LADY.
A BIT OF IRISH SCENERY.

PART III.

THE QUEEN'S ADVICE TO THE LORD
LIEUTENANT
(OVERHEARD AND RELATED BY
MURPHY THE SLATER).
THE CHILDREN'S PARTY, AS DESCRIBED
BY THE REV. PETER BINKS.

And Mr. French's latest success, a Quick-
Change Sketch, á la Biondi,
In which Mr. French will impersonate

M. LOUIS DE ROUGEMONT

And Recount one of his Authentic
Adventures.

TO CONCLUDE WITH A SOLO ON
THE CINEMATOGRAPH.

In a batch of songs to appear during the year was also **Flaherty's Drake.**

The Quick-Change Company, with Alice Lindé (the go-between)
and his wife Lennie helping him in the wings with the changes.
(See previous page for programme details.)

Russell & Sons
PALMER STREET, W.
13, HIGH STREET WINDSOR.
PHOTOGRAPHERS BY APPOINTMENT TO H.M. THE QUEEN.

Savage Club Supper.

JUNE 9TH, 1899.

● ● ●

...MENU...

Soup.
—
ASPARAGUS.
=
Fish.
—
MAYONNAISE OF SALMON.
=
Cold Joints.
—
ROAST LAMB.   MINT SAUCE.
SALAD.
ROAST RIBS OF BEEF.
HORSERADISH SAUCE.
=
Sweets.
—
FRENCH FINGER PASTRY.
PINE APPLE CREAMS.
WINE JELLIES.
—
PARMESAN STRAWS.

By now French was making occasional appearances in England, where he lodged in Chelsea. In 1899, aged 45, he gave a series of recitals in London, and was persuaded to move there by his agent, Gerald Christie. In the winter of 1899/1900 the French family moved into 21 Clifton Hill, in St. John's Wood.

Sketch of Mark Twain drawn on the edge of a menu.

French loved painting skies, which are usually the centre of interest in his watercolours. The wide open landscapes of his native Roscommon and the vivid sunsets of his Cavan years helped to concentrate his interest.

CELESTIAL PAINTING

When painters leave this world, we grieve
For the hand that will work no more,
But who can say that they rest alway
On that still celestial shore?
No! no! they choose from the rainbow hues,
And, winging from Paradise,
They come to paint, now bold, now faint,
The tones of our sunset skies.
When I see them there I can almost swear
That grey is from Whistler's brain!
That crimson flush is Turner's brush!
And the gold is Claude Lorraine!

*As gifts, French put together
little albums of paintings and poems,
with the watercolours matching the verses.*

CHAPTER FOUR:

LONDON

Oh, Mary, this London's a wonderful sight,
Wid the people here workin' by day and by night:
They don't sow potatoes, nor barley, nor wheat,
But there's gangs o' them diggin' for gold in the street –
At least, when I axed them, that's what I was told,
So I just took a hand at this diggin' for gold,
But for all that I found there, I might as well be
Where the Mountains o' Mourne sweep down to the sea.

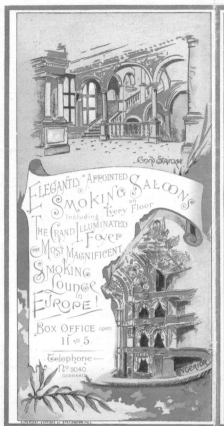

His first appearance on the London variety stage.

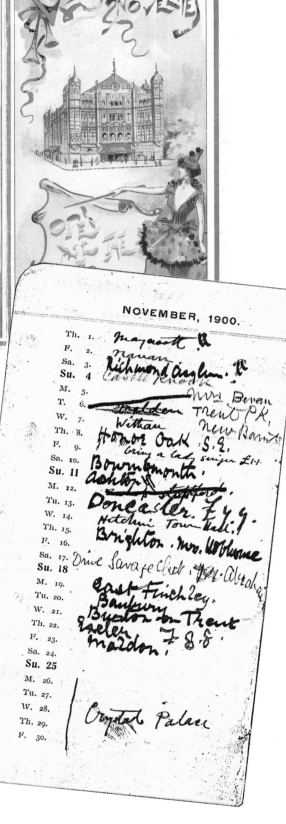

Engagement diaries were kept by his wife.

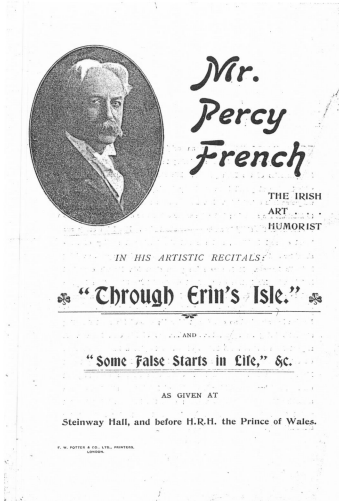

A sample of the publicity material that French sent to potential promoters.

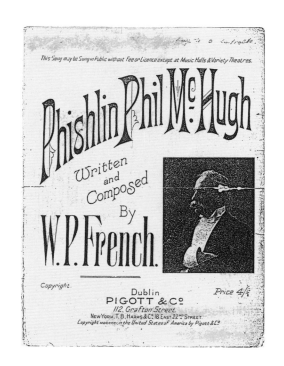

BIOGRAPHICAL PARTICULARS.

Mr. PERCY FRENCH is an original humorist who has spent many years of his life painting the scenery and studying the idiosyncracies of the Irish peasant. His store of anecdote and facility with brush and pencil have gradually developed a lecture which is as unique as it is entertaining. Mr. French does not rely on lantern slides to illustrate his remarks; but with water colours or charcoal he produces the scenes of the story in an incredibly short time. His Irish songs are based on real incidents, and are not the incoherent medley of man-slaughter and whisky which London is too prone to look upon as voicing Ireland's humour. It is now some years since Mr. French convulsed Dublin with his lecture on "Ireland up to date." Since then he has had to appear in every Irish town of note; and his name on a concert programme always attracts a crowded house. His astonishing success in London has surprised no one except himself; one of his most diverting attributes being an apparent unconsciousness of his own humour. A request from H. R. H. the Prince of Wales to give a humorous lecture on art (with illustrations) was the first intimation Mr. French got that his reputation had preceded him. Since then he has been in great demand, and has proved himself capable of holding the attention of even a fashionable drawing-room audience; even the tea-room being deserted whilst the lecturer performs the unique feat of talking and painting simultaneously.

THE TATLER   [No. 3, July 17 1901

HOW I MAKE SMOKE PICTURES.
By Percy French.

AN EASY EFFECT TO BE OBTAINED ON A SMOKED PLATE

The requirements for the manufacture of a smoke picture can be found in every household. No studio is required, no paint box, no easel, no brush, merely a candle, a box of wooden matches, and a white china plate. Place the lighted candle on a table in a position free from draughts, and sharpen one end of a match with a penknife. Hold the plate for a few seconds horizontally over and touching the candle flame; this will produce a deep dark smudge in the centre of the plate. On this draw with your sharpened match the outline of your deepest dark, whether rock, boat, or clump of trees, and wipe away all the surrounding blackness. Now if a mountain range is required at the back of the picture, bring the plate up to the candle, and pausing until the flame ceases to flicker, then pass the plate quickly and at an angle across the flame. This should leave a light band of smoke across the picture. The full strength should not be tried for at first, as the clouds being superimposed would make the finished picture too dark. This process may have made a misty mountain of about the required size and tone, but the experiment may result in a series of black marks or an aurora borealis of streaks; in this case it should be rubbed out and tried again.

The mountain having been delineated the outline may be made a little sharper by rubbing it with the finger, but if the smoke has left it fairly defined it had better be left alone. Definition sometimes gives strength, but if used in the distance is liable to destroy atmosphere. The sky is the next thing to attack. Hold the plate almost perpendicularly against the flame and sweep it quickly across in a horizontal direction; the result should be a cloud partially veiling the tops of the mountains; and lastly, with the sharpened end of a match, the high lights may be pricked out. It will soon be discovered how much the effect depends on the right "value" of the half-tones and how two deep darks or two high lights of equal strength nullify each other. Everything else depends on practice and skill.

Smoke pictures have been brought to great perfection by several German artists whose works command very high prices in Germany. The British public are as yet a little doubtful as to the precise place of this curious medium among the decorative arts. If the student adds a fine sable brush and a bottle of Indian ink (mixed with vandyke brown) to his outfit he can study composition to his heart's content. The picture can be preserved by pouring varnish known as "Soehnée Frères" over them.

EVERY PICTURE ON THIS PAGE WAS MADE WITH ONLY A PIECE OF PORCELAIN, A MATCH, AND A CANDLE

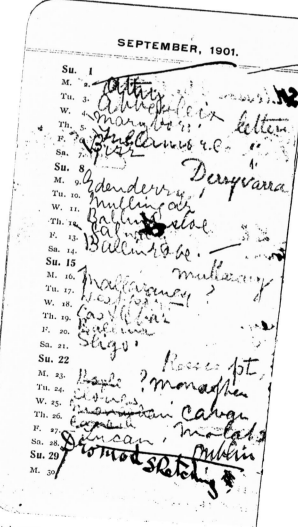

ARE YE RIGHT THERE, MICHAEL?

WORDS BY
PERCY FRENCH.

MUSIC BY
W. H. COLLISSON.

POPULAR SONGS ILLUSTRATED.

DUBLIN:
PIGOTT & CO.,
112, GRAFTON STREET.

COPYRIGHT. Copyright MDCCCCII. in the United States of America by PIGOTT & CO.

PRICE 2/-

Are ye right there, Michael?

The music was originally by Collisson, but later replaced by a tune composed by French himself.

The West Clare Railway incident finally surfaced in song.

'Are ye right there, Michael, are ye right?
Do you think that we'll be there before the night?
Ye've been so long in startin',
That ye couldn't say for sartin' –
Still ye might now, Michael, so ye might'.

Where are you for, man? Kilrush? Change at Moyasta Junction. Coming back to-night? – let me see if there's a train – 6.30, Saturdays only 8.00. Ay! if the Express is over an hour late you'll just catch it. Tickets ready! Tickets – lost your ticket! where are ye for? – Galway! – yer in the wrong train, man! Over the bridge with ye. Run, ye duck legged nonentity – that's right, break yer neck! Howld on there Peter, there's another passenger for ye! Bedad he'd have missed the train if he hadn't slipped on the top of the stairs. (Sung) While you're waiting in the train, ye'll hear the guard sing this refrain. Are ye right there, Michael, are ye right?

My dear litte Mollie
I hope you are jolly, and
not melancholly, for that
would & be folly

Is Violet's nose, still where
the nose grows, has she lost
all her clothes, and the rest
of her toes.

I hope that the cat is both
happy and fat, and you
dont squash her flat when
you sit on the mat.

Now don't be a baddie,
for that makes me saddie,
be good and I'm gladdie
your loving
old
DADDIE

SEPTEMBER, 1901.

Irish tour

41

Although French never talked about the death of his first wife, it is quite likely that this tragic loss inspired some of his 'pathetic poems' (as he called them), such as Gortnamona and the ones printed on pages 19 and 20. Gortnamona is an estate near Tullamore in County Offaly. French was a friend of the O'Connor-Morris family that lived there.

GORTNAMONA

Long, long ago in the woods of Gortnamona,
I thought the birds were singing in the Blackthorn tree;
But oh, it was my heart that was ringing, ringing, ringing,
With the joy that you were bringing, O my love, to me.

Long, long ago, in the woods of Gortnamona,
I thought the wind was sighing round the Blackthorn tree;
But oh, it was the Banshee that was crying, crying, crying,
And I knew my love was dying far across the sea.

Now if you go through the woods of Gortnamona,
You hear the raindrops creeping through the Blackthorn tree.
But oh, it is the tears I am weeping, weeping, weeping,
For the loved one that is sleeping far away from me.

Programme for 1902.

WHY DON'T WE ALL DRAW.

My First Portrait.

The Ballad of Ann and the Baker's Young Man.

A Revolution in Sea Painting.

The Man of Letters.

＋❊❊＋

THE PAVEMENT ARTIST'S STORY.

A Study in Curves.

The Art of the Reciter.

＋❊❊＋

A DAY WITH ANDY GERAGHTY.

The Sequel to the King of the Otters.

The Concert in Crahage.

＋❊❊＋

A KERRY COURTHOUSE.

Sweeny *v.* McHugh and others.

＋❊❊＋

MY GREAT PANORAMA (SECOND EDITION)

Of Places I haven't seen.

Illustrated by Sketches drawn on the Spot.

＋❊❊＋

A FEW WORDS ON ZOOLOGY.

With an Illustration of the Sad Story of the Elephant and Hen.

＋❊❊＋

A LAY OF THE WILD WEST CLARE.

＋❊❊＋

MY SKETCHING CLASS.

A Lesson in Landscape and Love.

RECENT PRESS NOTICES.

"Mr. Percy French, who gave a recital at the Steinway Hall yesterday afternoon, is a single-handed entertainer who takes quite a line of his own. Give him a few sheets of brown paper and a handful of coloured chalks, and he can keep his audience amused by the hour and more with his lightning sketches and other pictorial funniments. Now it is "Art in the Nursery" which is illustrated (Young Hopeful's early efforts with pen and pencil), then some Irish reminiscences (including an illustration of the wonderful apparition which Andy saw in Donegal); later, the "story of a pot-boiler" (showing with what success a rising young artist turned a picture of still life into a Turneresque seascape), and so on —the products in each instance being highly ingenious and diverting. In short, His talk, too, is excellent—both the lightning sketching Mr. French is an indubitable master. recitations, anecdotes, and the like with which he intersperses his drawings and his recital of his experiences as an adult at a children's party fairly convulsed his hearers. In a word, one can pass a very amusing hour indeed in Mr. French's company.—*Westminster Gazette.*

Mr. Percy French's Fun.—Since the lamented death of Corney Grain London has sadly needed a single-handed entertainer of real originality and humour. Mr. Percy French is quite capable of filling the vacant place, and as his excellent entertainments become more generally known in London he will quite certainly attain widespread popularity. Mr. French's humour is thoroughly typical of his native Ireland, though it is not of the boisterous order and is entirely devoid of any trace of vulgarity. Nothing indeed could be more original or more racy than his rapid illustrations in chalk of his amusing stories, parodies and conceits. While he befools his audience with funny chatter about "the early Victorian poem, 'Hey Diddle, Diddle,'" the cat appears on the easel with a few bold strokes of the chalk; a few more add the "fiddle," and the drawing is then turned upside down when, lo and behold!—there is the cow and the moon that it jumped over. A little clever shading is added, and a second reversing of the paper presents the laughing dog to an audience that is by this time in the same condition only more so. In similar fashion "My Great Panorama" shows a series of rapid transformation of a view of "London from the Tower" into the Eddystone Lighthouse, the Great Pyramid, the Matterhorn and so on, accompanied by inimitably droll comment full of flashes of dry wit. And while the quality of the fun is always first-rate, the manner of its expression is constantly varied. At one moment we have exceedingly clever parodies of style showing what "Goosey Goosey Gander" would have been if written by Swinburne, Longfellow, and Kipling; at another, laughable chalk pictures drawn in an instant of types of females and of the surprising husbands with whom they mated, proving the mutual attraction of opposites. And finally, such is Mr. French's versatility, he exchanges the chalk for the banjo and sings some of his own delightful Irish songs with quaint humour.—*St. James' Gazette.*

"Mr. Percy French gives a clever representation of rapid chalk sketches, which are executed while he is describing the scene they are supposed to represent, and the puzzled audience wonders what the drawing will be, until he reverses the paper and they find that it has been sketched upside down, and that, placed in a proper position, it is a really artistic piece of work. We have not been able to do more than indicate a very few of the various items which render this entertainment genuinely attractive, and we commend it especially to the clergy and their families.—*Church Bells.*

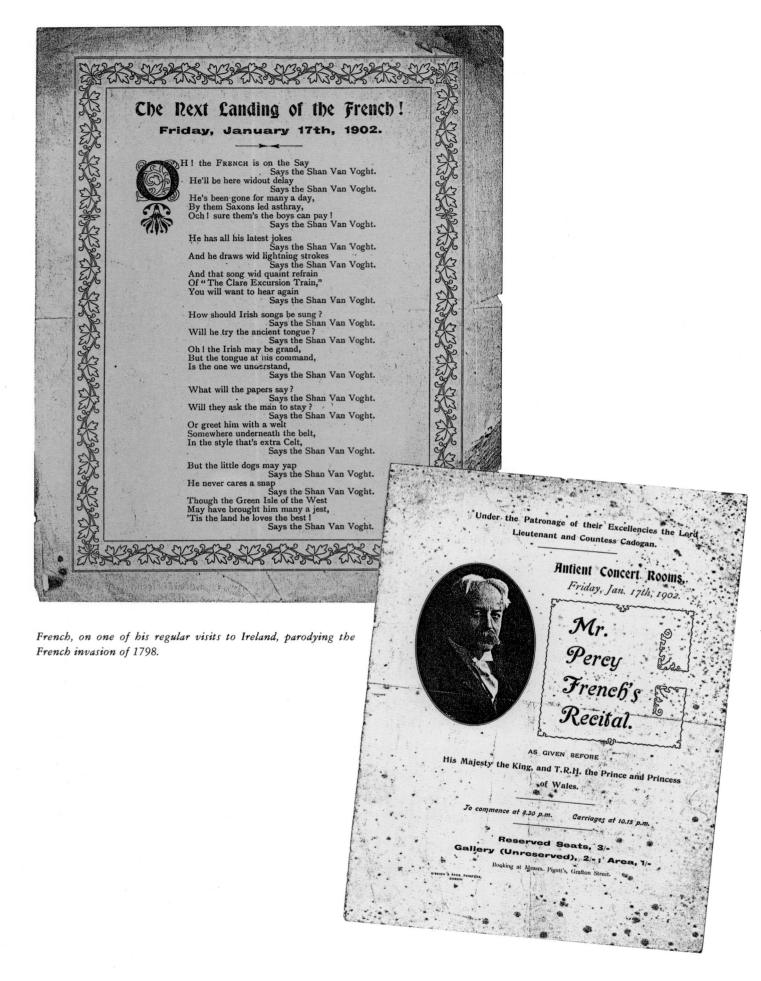

The Next Landing of the French!
Friday, January 17th, 1902.

OH! the FRENCH is on the Say
        Says the Shan Van Voght.
He'll be here widout delay
        Says the Shan Van Voght.
He's been-gone for many a day,
By them Saxons led asthray,
Och! sure them's the boys can pay!
        Says the Shan Van Voght.

He has all his latest jokes
        Says the Shan Van Voght.
And he draws wid lightning strokes
        Says the Shan Van Voght.
And that song wid quaint refrain
Of " The Clare Excursion Train,"
You will want to hear again
        Says the Shan Van Voght.

How should Irish songs be sung?
        Says the Shan Van Voght.
Will he try the ancient tongue?
        Says the Shan Van Voght.
Oh! the Irish may be grand,
But the tongue at his command,
Is the one we unaerstand,
        Says the Shan Van Voght.

What will the papers say?
        Says the Shan Van Voght.
Will they ask the man to stay?
        Says the Shan Van Voght.
Or greet him with a welt
Somewhere underneath the belt,
In the style that's extra Celt,
        Says the Shan Van Voght.

But the little dogs may yap
        Says the Shan Van Voght.
He never cares a snap
        Says the Shan Van Voght.
Though the Green Isle of the West
May have brought him many a jest,
'Tis the land he loves the best!
        Says the Shan Van Voght.

French, on one of his regular visits to Ireland, parodying the French invasion of 1798.

Under the Patronage of their Excellencies the Lord Lieutenant and Countess Cadogan.

Antient Concert Rooms,
Friday, Jan. 17th, 1902.

Mr. Percy French's Recital.

AS GIVEN BEFORE
His Majesty the King, and T.R.H. the Prince and Princess of Wales.

To commence at 8.30 p.m.   *Carriages at 10.15 p.m.*

Reserved Seats, 3/-
Gallery (Unreserved), 2/- ; Area, 1/-

Booking at Messrs. Pigott's, Grafton Street.

O'BRIEN & ARDS, PRINTERS, DUBLIN.

THE END OF THE HOLIDAY

Fold up the box, the wind is chill,
The hills are turning grey,
To-morrow I must pay my bill,
And speed me far away,
Back to the world again - but still
Thank God for such a day.

Ettie, painted on one of the family holidays in Brittany.

From Dublin, where he gave the programme announced opposite,
French sent letters to the children at home in London.

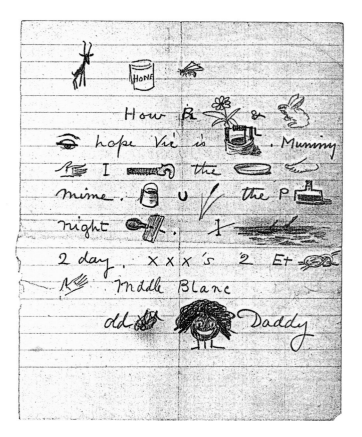

Sunday

Dear Ettie, I got a great many pennies in Dublin. I am sailing in a ship to Glasgow, a town in Scotland. I saw your letter to Granny. I liked the cats very much. Your loving Daddy.

Dear Honeybee, how are Daisy and Bunny? I hope Vic is well. Mummy and I saw the pantomime. Can you read the Pink Night Owl: I cross the sea to-day. Kisses to Ettie and Mlle Blanc.

Looking at the range of the Mourne Mountains from Skerries one clear afternoon I found myself repeating 'The Mountains of Mourne sweep down to the sea.' This line kept recurring to me till one day it wedded itself to an old Irish air, and the combination seemed so happy that I set to work, or rather shut myself in my top room with pen, ink and paper, and waited. Presently the idea entered my head that such a refrain might be sung by an exile from Erin - Lord Northcliffe's dictum that you interest the greatest number of people if you talk about love, or about London, also occurred to me at the time; and so my most successful song, admirably arranged by Dr Collisson, was given to an applauding public.

THE MOUNTAINS O' MOURNE.

1.

Oh, Mary, this London's a wonderful sight,
Wid the people here workin' by day and by night;
They don't sow potatoes, nor barley, nor wheat,
But there's gangs o' them diggin' for gold in the street—
At least, when I axed them, that's what I was told,
So I just took a hand at this diggin' for gold,
But for all that I found there I might as well be
Where the Mountains o' Mourne sweep down to the sea.

2.

I believe that, when writin', a wish you expressed
As to how the fine ladies in London were dressed.
Well, if you'll believe me, when axed to a ball,
They don't wear a top to their dresses at all.
Oh, I've seen them meself, and you could not, in thrath,
Say if they were bound for a ball or a bath—
Don't be startin' them fashions now, Mary Macree,
Where the Mountains o' Mourne sweep down to the sea.

3.

I seen England's King from the top of a 'bus—
I never knew him, though he means to know us;
And though by the Saxon we once were oppressed,
Still, I cheered—God forgive me!—I cheered wid the rest.
And now that he's visited Erin's green shore,
We'll be much better friends than we've been heretofore,
When we've got all we want we're as quiet as can be
Where the Mountains o' Mourne sweep down to the sea.

4.

You remember young Peter O'Loughlin, of course—
Well, here he is here at the head o' the Force.
I met him to-day, I was crossing the Strand,
And he stopped the whole street wid wan wave of his hand;
And there we stood talking of days that are gone,
While the whole population of London looked on;
But for all these great powers he's wishful, like me,
To be back where dark Mourne sweeps down to the sea.

5.

There's beautiful girls here—oh, never mind!
Wid beautiful shapes Nature never designed,
And lovely complexions, all roses and crame,
But O'Loughlin remarked wid regard to them same:
" That if at those roses you venture to sip,
The colours might all come away on your lip,"
So I'll wait for the wild rose that's waitin' for me
Where the Mountains o' Mourne sweep down to the sea.

21. CLIFTON HILL. LONDON, N.W.   PERCY FRENCH.

The first printed song copy shows clearly that the song was written in exile in London.

21 Clifton Hill

HOME LIFE

I'm sure we had a very happy childhood unencumbered by the elaborate toys, T.V. and early school of today's children. We played on the floor with a box of bricks and a pack of cards that served both for playing games and building card houses, and, most exciting of all, behind the closed doors of the dining room we could hear people singing and playing the banjo, and sometimes even having a fencing match as we could hear the clash of rapiers, and once when the door was open a chink we looked through and saw a man walking on his hands! Our lives were ordered with mild discipline by Mummy and Nanny, while Daddy was a visitor who came when we were in bed and told stories, extempore rhymes, and made shadow pictures on the wall opposite the nursery fire.

The pattern changed when we moved to London, where Daddy's quick rise to fame as an entertainer kept him busy and often away overnight. I think Mummy would have liked to have become a society hostess, but her efforts were thwarted because his spare time had to be spent in his studio writing and rehearsing his compositions, which were all original and had to be new for every new season. When visitors came Daddy would appear after urgent calls, banjo in hand, rehearse his latest number, ask their opinion and disappear again saying he had much work to do.

When we came to England, Daddy's Irish children with their Scottish Nanny became two little English girls with a French Nursery Governess. Mollie and I skipped around before our school days and I remember a truly awful game we used to play after lunch. It was called Thumpy Thatch, and it consisted of frogs leaping all round the table when we were full of food and high spirits, and we used to get dear Daddy, who was nearly fifty at that time, to join us, with one of us in front and the other behind, and leap round and round until one of us was exhausted and had to fall out.

(Ettie French, daughter)

TO ETTS & MOLLS

I go to bed just when I like,
I seldom brush my hair,
I've got a banjo and a bike,
I *should* be free from care.

No nurse to button on my clothes
Or put soap in mine eye,
I've got a watch that really goes –
And yet I sometimes sigh.

I cannot yell the livelong day
Nor dance the evening through,
In fact I'd sooner work than play –
How strange this seems to you.

You do not hear the wolves that creep
Around the house at night.
They only come when you're asleep
And nurse puts out the light.

But I can hear them snook and snuff
While doors and windows creak.
It takes four 'calls' of comic stuff
To slay them every week.

So if I seem lethargic at
The game of 'Jumping Frog,'
If I am crusty with the cat
Or seem to snub the dog,

Or if at 'Thumpy' you perceive
A dull and moody tone,
Remember, little ones, that we've
Got worries of our own.

On 26th April a third daughter
was born, Joan Phyllis.

His ambition was to write a successful play that would provide
him with an income and allow him more time to paint.

Around the time of Joan's birth French had to look after his own
engagement diaries for a while. From autumn to spring was a
round of engagements for schools and lecture societies, then came
the London season with its parties and functions, and finally the
Irish seaside tour in the summer holiday months.

Some years ago I was sketching in the wilds of Donegal, when an old woman came out of a cottage with 'a cup o' tay and a bite o' griddle cake for the dissolute stranger who was sittin' out like a shnipe in the bog.' Getting into conversation, she told me that all her boys and girls had gone to America, 'an' 'twas a lonely land to live in whin the childher was away.' This line haunted me all that afternoon, and that night in the little hotel at Falcarragh I wrote *'An Irish Mother.'*

Evening in Achill

AN IRISH MOTHER

A wee slip drawin' water,
Me ould man at the plough,
No grown-up son or daughter,
That's the way we're farmin' now.
'No work and little pleasure'
Was the cry before they wint,
Now they're gettin' both full measure,
So I ought to be contint.
Great wages men is givin'
In that land beyant the say,
But 'tis lonely - lonely livin'
Whin the childher is away.

Och, the baby in the cradle,
Blue eyes and curlin' hair,
God knows I'd give a gra'dle
To have little Pether there;
I doubt he'd think it funny
Lyin' here upon me arm,
Him that's earnin' the good money
On a Californy farm.
Six pounds it was, or sivin
He sint last quarther day,
But 'tis lonely, lonely livin'
Whin the childher is away.

God is good - none betther,
And the divil might be worse,
Each month there comes a letther
Bringing somethin' for the purse.
And me ould man's heart rejoices
Whin I read they're doin' fine,
But it's oh to hear their voices,
And to feel their hands in mine.
To see the cattle driven
And the young ones makin' hay,
'Tis a lonely land to live in
Whin the childher is away.

Whin the shadders do be fallin'
On the ould man there an' me,
'Tis hard to keep from callin'
'Come in childher to yer tea'
I can almost hear them comin'
Mary, Kate and little Con -
Och! but I'm the foolish woman,
Sure they're all grown up an' gone.
That our sins may be forgiven,
An' not wan go asthray,
I doubt I'd stay in Hivin
If thim childher was away.

PROGRAMME.

Matinee Recital.

PART I.

SOME STUDIES IN HISTORY
(By my youngest hope)
Mr. Percy French

THE GENTLE ART OF SHOPPING
Ernest Denny
(Some adventures in Bond Street)
Mr. Ernest Denny

HOW I BECAME A SCENE-PAINTER
Mr. Percy French

(a) MANDALAY ... *Rudyard Kipling*
(b) HUMOURS OF A SMART WEDDING
Anstey
Mr. Ernest Denny

Interval of Five Minutes

PART II.

HOW PETER BINKS TRIED TO CONJURE
AT A CHILDREN'S PARTY.
Mr. Percy French

SOMEBODY ELSE. A Tale of a Tea Shop.
Mr. Ernest Denny

HOW MAGUIRE PLAYED AT "GOFF."
Mr. Percy French

(a) SOME FABLES UP-TO-DATE ... *Anon*
"The woman who couldn't help herself"
"The woman who adapted herself"
(b) MY BROTHER SAM ... *Anon*
Mr. Ernest Denny

AN AMERICAN CHASER
Mr. Percy French

Evening Recital.

PART I.

EARLY EFFORTS IN ART
Mr. Percy French

THE TRUTH ABOUT TRAINS AND
TRAVELLERS ... *Ernest Denny*
(Being some humours and ill-humours of the
Railway)
Mr. Ernest Denny

HOW E. A. POE, TENNYSON, BURNS, AND
KIPLING WOULD HAVE WRITTEN
THE NURSERY RHYMES
Mr. Percy French

SNAPSHOTS IN STAGELAND ... *Jerome*
Mr. Ernest Denny

Interval of Five Minutes.

PART II.

ME FRIEND FINNEGAN
"How did they know that I came from Cork?"
Mr. Percy French

THE PERILS OF THE POST-
OFFICE } *Adapted from "Punch" by Ernest Denny*
The people who brave them and the
people who suffer them
Mr. Ernest Denny

A REVOLUTION IN SEA PAINTING
Mr. Percy French

(a) MORE FABLES UP-TO-DATE ... *Anon*
"The woman who helped her husband"
"The woman who wasn't athletic"
(b) RUBENSTEIN'S PIANO AND WHAT HE
DID WITH IT ... *Adams*
Mr. Ernest Denny

ANOTHER AMERICAN CHASER
Mr. Percy French

"Mr. Percy French's recitals are always a delight. They are, moreover, if his programme may be trusted, a joy to his landlord and various deserving tradesmen, his very faithful and confiding servants. But it is as humorist, musician, artist, rather than as purveyor to the entertainment of such gentry, that he makes his strongest appeal to the public. And yesterday afternoon, as befitted the occasion, a large number of these latter assembled at the Steinway Hall to do him honour, and, incidentally, to draw two hours solid amusement from his shrewd remarks and brilliant performance with pencil and paper. To follow him step by step through his long and varied programme would demand more space, not, we hasten to say, than the subject deserves, but than the obtrusive presence of, from his standpoint, less important matters admits of giving to it. Enough that yesterday Mr. French was at his best, and from first to last kept his listeners in a state of mirthful and wrapt attention. Of all his sketches the last, "The Evolution of Hiawatha," proved to be the best, and served abundantly to show how entirely needless was the printed caution that "Contributions of fruit, vegetables, eggs, etc., must be left with the doorkeeper, and not be thrown at the entertainer."—*Daily Telegraph*, June 17th, 1904.

"That Mr. Percy French has a large *clientele* was apparent by the large audience that filled the Steinway Hall yesterday afternoon, on the occasion of his only public recital this season. Mr. French presented a programme of almost entirely new sketches and in all of these his genial wit and refined humour drew unstinted applause from his hearers. An excellent example of his style was to be found in the foreword upon his programme, which explained that "the bulk of the proceeds will go to the support of Mr. French's landlord and other deserving tradesmen; the remainder forming a reserve fund for the tax collector, as this unhappy individual suffers from hallucinations, chiefly on the subject of Mr. French's alleged wealth." Quite the best of his contributions yesterday was that which told how Peter Binks turned conjuror to amuse his little friends—a sketch built on the lines of his popular "Lion" story, in which the imaginary crowd of children ask pertinent questions, to the great discomfort of the performer. Mr. French's sketches in coloured chalks proved as effective and as surprising as ever, and as an afternoon's entertainment, the recital proved entirely to the taste of all who were present."
Standard, June 17th, 1904.

The *Court Circular* of December 19th, 1902, says—" Mr. French brings a wealth of quiet Irish humour to bear in his unceasing flow of anecdote and comment, which he pours out the while he sketches pictures in chalk with marvellous rapidity, sometimes turning his canvas upside down at the finish, so as to give his audience two pictures instead of one. This versatile artist can also sing—he was the composer of "The Sons of the Prophet"—and provokes uncontrollable laughter by his clever dialogues with imaginary children, whose remarks, like those of Mr. Caudle, are never heard, but suggested."

Achill Sound

THE ISLAND OF MY DREAMS

This London sky is dull and grey;
A storm of sleet and rain
Is beating dismally to-day
Upon my window pane.
On wings of fancy let me stray
To summer shores again.

Once more the fresh Atlantic breeze
Its friendly greeting cries;
Afar across the azure seas
The cliffs of Achill rise,
And cloudland's countless pageantries
Sweep thro' the sunlit skies.

The distance fills with misty hills,
Alternate gleam and gloom;
I see again the purple plain
Bestarred with golden broom,
Whilst at my feet the meadowsweet
Pours fourth its faint perfume.

So when along the Achill Sound
The summer sunset gleams,
And when the heatherbells are found
Beside the mountain streams,
I'll seek thy shore and live once more,
O island of my dreams.

In January 1905 the French family moved nearby to 48 Springfield Road.

A French Immigrant. *With hat turned inside out, French posed for the camera.*

Joan's birth brought the next change. She was too young to share in her sisters' amusements, but Daddy constructed a stage in the drawing room, complete with curtains and painted backcloth, for the performance of plays and entertainments by herself and her small friends. The first show was Tableaux, and between each one there was a long, long pause for the changing of clothes, during which Daddy and Hill Rowan, a member of the Magic Circle, entertained the audience with card tricks. Now over fifty and comfortably off, he could relax and enjoy the company of the children he loved, and he put a little easel in his studio for Joan.

(Ettie French, daughter)

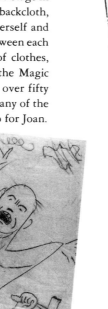

'A WRYME AND A WRIGGLE'

There was an old man of Kilcoole
Who married a wife, quite a fool.
''Twas a union,' he'd say,
'That I wanted that day,
But begorrah I'm getting Home Rule!'

In the first half French would invite one of the audience to provide a word and a squiggle of chalk on paper. The key word in this case was Kilcoole. By the second half French had composed a limerick, which he would recite while completing the picture.

NOVELTY AT THE PRINCE'S.

It will be well to provide a name for the at present unchristened piece presented for the first time on any stage at the Prince's Theatre, Manchester, last night. To that conclusion we were led on witnessing its initial appearance. This preliminary deficiency is to be remedied by Manchester theatre-goers, a prize being offered for the best title submitted up to Saturday night. Described "as a musical costume comedy," the term aptly describes the play, the "book" of which is by Mr. Frank Barrett, the lyrics by Mr. Percy French, and the music by Mr. J. A. Robertson, who composed the score of "Winnie Brooke." To say that Miss Ada Reeve is in the cast, and that she has a part which affords abundant scope for the exercise of her versatile powers, is at once to ensure interest in the production. It is a distinctly pleasing play, and was enjoyed by a large audience last night. There is something more than a mere pretence in the construction of the story, and as it proceeds one finds oneself awaiting the denouement with considerable interest. n. her father Dick Dawson

Another musical comedy appeared.

From the National Press Agency Ltd.

CHUCKLES IN CHALK.

HINTS FOR A UNIQUE CHRISTMAS ENTERTAINMENT.

By PERCY FRENCH.

"I am going," said our curate, "to read a selection from Dickens's works to my poor women."

"Poor women!" I muttered, sympathetically."

"You are afraid Dickens won't interest them?" he queried.

No, I said, he will not. Dickens didn't write for the platform. Give them something they can grasp the meaning of. Know anything about babies?"

"Not as yet," said the curate.

I remembered his but recently-announced engagement and apologised.

"I wish you would come down and help me to amuse the old ladies," he said. "Oh, if you could only make them laugh!"

"I'll come," I replied – "gladly. And I'll try and make them laugh," I added grimly, "but it must be after they've been fed. No living entertainer could face them before they've had their tea. I shall want a blackboard and easel, and do try and keep the light *on* me and *off* the audience. Amateurs never realise how the lighting affects the success of their entertainments."

"I don't quite see –" begged the curate.

"A picture on cardboard taken from the schoolroom wall, and fastened to the gas-bracket, or hung on the lamp on the side next the audience will do it. And now tell me the way to the nearest oil and colour man."

In half an hour I had all I wanted. My necessaries were a couple of lumps of "drop black" (3d.), a small piece of whiting (½d.), a quire of unglazed wrapping-paper from the grocer (3d.), and a few screw-eyes from the ironmonger (2d.). I then devoted ten minutes to carefully drawing these two heads, and, putting a sheet of paper over them, walked down to the schoolhouse.

I found my audience silently awaiting my arrival, and a glance at the old ladies shewed me that my work was cut out for me. Solemnly they gazed on me whilst I fastened my quire of paper to the board with the screw-eyes. Sternly they frowned upon me as I turned and faced them, armed only with a lump of drop black and a piece of whiting.

"My subject," I said, "is 'Babies,' and let me here shew you a couple of baldheaded babes for whom I and I alone am responsible."

Here I pulled off my cover-paper and revealed the above-mentioned babes.

(Note.– The hair should be put on after the babes are shewn and not before, as I have done it here.)

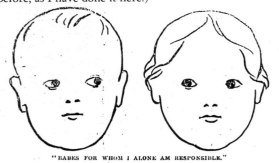

"BABES FOR WHOM I ALONE AM RESPONSIBLE."

"Now the father is never so much interested in small babies as the mother is so I am going to make these two grow up as quickly as possible."

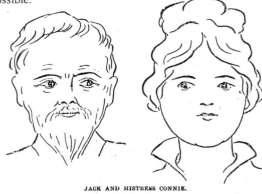

JACK AND MISTRESS CONNIE.

I then recited a ballad, and as I did so added the appropriate touches with black and white chalk, till I reached the final tableau of Darby and Joan.

DARBY AND JOAN.

I said I would now give them my reasons for believing that little girls came from flowers.

"Take the daffodil," I said, "and observe its graceful lines; add a buttercup to it (the head), and see how attractive it becomes – the little flies come buzzing about it" (here I dotted in the eyes, nose, and mouth on the buttercup). "Then a bumble-bee comes along – you can only see its folded wings" (here I added the legs). "And here" (turning the board half round), "here we have Miss May Blossom all complete!"

Continuing the subject, I shewed them how the small boy was descended from the rabbit. This was a further surprise, as it necessitated the board being turned upside down, and an accidental likeness being discovered to "our Jimmy" rendered this work a triumph of art!

Then I challenge the company to a game of "Squiggles." This game, I explained, consists of giving a person a wriggly outline of any description, which he has there and then to convert into some recognisable object. A small boy gave me the first one, and only the fact of my having practised drawing and seeing things upside down, saved me from being beaten by the enigma I got on this occasion. As it was, a few lines made it into a passable boat, and I suggested to the organist that "A Life on the Ocean Wave" would be an appropriate melody on the piano.

I followed this up with an example of ambidextrous drawing. This is not hard to do, as you have only to think of the right hand, and the left hand will perform the same curves automatically.

The example I gave is known as the "Kissing Cup," and has had many variations since it was discovered in an early Greek painting. I, of course, drew the cup first (with both hands), and then shewed why it was called the Kissing Cup by finishing the profile heads.

THE EVOLUTION OF MISS MAY BL...

SHOWING HOW THE SMALL BOY IS DESCENDED FROM A RABBIT.

A "SQUIGGLE."

THE KISSING CUP.

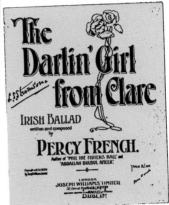

We were sittin' on the wall upon a Sunday
To watch the girls go by,
And thinkin' we'd be marrit to one one day
When Kate Flynn caught our eye.
Oh, Man! she was the makin's of a fairy,
And it made each boyo swear,
'There's not one girl in the wide, wide world
Like the girl from the County Clare!'

Golf! Golf! Carry me off!
Bury me down by the sea.
The lofters may loft,
Still my sleep shall be soft,
No more o' yer golfin' for me.

Whisper low!
When twilight shades are falling
Pull de clo' around de curly head
To and fro I hear de Hoodoo calling:
'Are dere any little picaninnies
who am not in bed?'

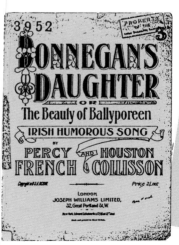

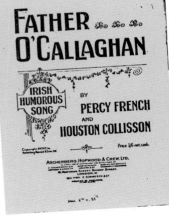

A bumper crop of songs.

A children's entertainment.

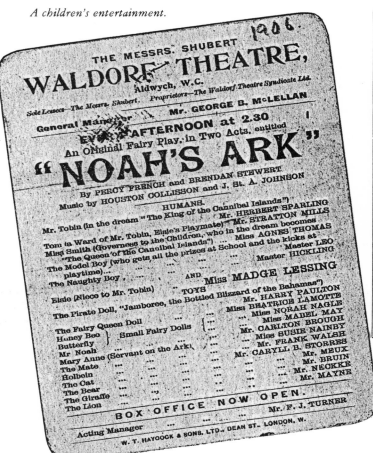

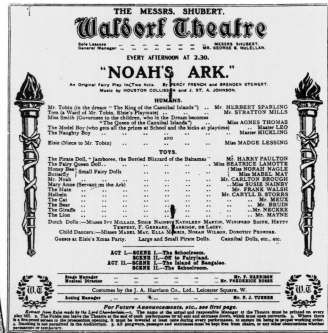

from THE GAMES WE PLAY

Now cricket's the game
Where I long to win fame,
Life, my friends, is a long game of cricket.
Be straight in your play,
Or you'll soon start away
To where Satan is keeping the wicked.
I go in last man, a praiseworthy plan,
If I score it's one chance in a million.
Then removing my hat
I carry my bat
And the stumps to the Cricket Pavilion.

BUILDING "NOAH'S ARK."

How Mr. French Wrote the Children's Play for the Waldorf.

On Saturday next the children of London will have "Noah's Ark" added to their Christmas entertainments at the Waldorf Theatre. To-day an "Evening News" representative saw Mr. Percy French, the author, and asked him how he came to write it. Mr. French said:—"After seeing 'The Tempest,' or 'Beauty and the Barge,' or some such play, the thought occurred to me how much better the nautical drama might be written if entrusted to really capable hands.

"Firstly I saw there must be in my story some well-known mariner, one whose name is a household word, as celebrated in the nursery as on the high seas.

"Columbus, Marco Polo, Basil Hall, Anson, and Sebastian Cabot were all mentioned to the baby without eliciting a spark of interest, but when I spoke of Noah the eyes lit up, the smile became almost twice life-size, and I knew my hero was found.

"I soon found that Noah refused to become more than a wooden dummy, and relegating him to the background, I began elaborating a ferocious pirate called Captain Jamboree, who converted the Ark into a fore-and-aft schooner, and set sail in search of buried treasure to the Cannibal Island of Bangaloo.

DR. COLLISSON'S VIEWS.

"It was at this point that I asked my friend Dr. Collisson to introduce some musical numbers, and my friend Brendan Stewart to assist me in the construction.

"Dr. Collisson suggested a scene in Piccadilly, with a chorus of pirate 'buses, and a dance for flower girls, also a snow scene in Hyde Park, with Noah feeding the ducks to a sort of 'Quack, quack' chorus off stage.

"Perhaps the best advice I got was from Mr. Stewart, who said, 'Write as many disconnected funny scenes as you like, and leave them to the producer, the leading lady, and the comedians. Also write songs which can be sung by the Fairy Queen or the Elephant, or given in dumb show by the Cannibals.'

"The telephone has played a conspicuous part in the genesis of 'Noah's Ark,' and many a time have I been summoned to the instrument and listened while Dr. Collisson buzzed or whistled some inspiration for song or duet in my ear.

"Oh, by-the-way, I was to have told you how I wrote this Christmas fantasy. Well, the fact is, it's not written—Excuse me—the telephone—that's Mr. Johnson I expect—he's doing the 'additional numbers' for us. 'Hello! Who's that?—Johnson?. Yes! Oh, they want to alter your moonlight serenade into a duet for two Hedgehogs. 'All right, I'll post it to-night!' 'Good-bye'!"

The Times.

The introduction of pirates into a fairy play is obviously a necessity if the play is to be appreciated by small boys, and the addition of a moral is no doubt found by experience to allay the fears of parents and maiden aunts. After seeing *Noah's Ark* little boys will not be driven to attempt any desperate adventures on the Round Pond, or any other place suitable for filibustering expeditions, and little girls will realize that, after all, a schoolroom has its attractions, even if they are not so great as those of a cannibal island. But, in spite of the moral, or possibly because of it, this fairy play is most entertaining, and Miss Madge Lessing and Mr. Stratton Mills make two most entertaining children. She wants to be a fairy and he to be a pirate (although he had been intended for holy orders and scorned his guardian's suggestion that he should split the difference and become a lawyer, which is "something between a pirate and a clergyman"), and so naturally they fall asleep and dream dreams. So they sail away on an ark, with a pirate captain and crew and Mr. Noah and his family and all the animals with square haunches and spotted flanks according to regulation, and arrive at the island where lies the buried treasure. The modern child prefers to think that the treasure is great store of chocolate, which is not so sordid as pieces of eight, but he will weep to hear that the crew are found and frightened away by the cannibals. Here the dream ends, and the fairy queen took the opportunity to preach Imperialism when we had suspected her, for no cause, of being a Little Englander; and in the schoolroom once again, when the dream is over, a children's party is given. It is all very good fun, and the little pirate tabloids who have to be incubated, and the fairies great and small, the cannibals, Uncle Tobin, and the governess, and the giraffe who ate Mr. Noah's stockings seemed greatly to please. There is one little fairy, about 3ft. high or less—we apologize if fairies should be measured by barleycorns or hands or anything less prosaic than feet—who is particularly delightful and who should become a great actress if she is not spoilt; but then all modern children are spoilt or they would not have such amusing plays produced for their own special benefit.

THE DIRGE OF THE DAUGHTERS

We've a house in Eaton Square,
We've the entrée everywhere,
To look upon we're not at all unpleasant.
We used to entertain,
And perhaps we may again,
But we're keeping rather quiet for the present.

It's not that we've been rash
In investing any cash,
It's not that we are weary of the season,
We delight in fun and feast,
We're not blasé, not the least,
But *Mother's playing Bridge,* and that's the reason.

We were happy months ago,
'Darling Maud and dearest Flo,
You are always such a comfort to your Mummy.'
That was how it used to be,
But since Bridge appeared – ah me!
We haven't been conspicuously chummy.

Mother's temper's getting worse,
Getting short – and so's her purse –
I wouldn't be the one to disobey her,
We wouldn't care a bit
If 'twas but a passing fit,
But Mother rather fancies she's a player.

If one wants to buy a hat
Or some trifling thing like that,
She's got to settle up for last night's looting,
If we 'settle *down*' again,
It will not be near Park Lane,
I incline to Shepherd's Bush or Upper Tooting.

For she rarely, rarely, wins,
Oh she suffers for her sins,
And I.O.U.s accumulate upon her.
The players whom she meets,
She knows are mostly cheats,
And still she will refer to 'debts of Honour.'

Ah, the bitterness and shame,
In this soul destroying game,
The energy and time they waste upon it.
We have got no Mother now,
And we never shall, I vow,
While this very latest B is in her bonnet.

Don't call this a fancy sketch
For I know a girl – poor wretch
Who's living now on Fortune's lowest level,
And another who was told
They'd not take her Mother's gold
If she – Bridge! I know your name now, it's the Devil!

THE FOOLISH LITTLE FROG
BY PERCY FRENCH
ILLUSTRATED BY JOHN HASSALL.

Invasion of Chelsea
by the French !

Panic among the Inhabitants ! !

Men, Women & Children
taken off

Date of Invasion fixed for Feb. 15th
TOWN HALL ALREADY TAKEN
See Proclamation at Town Hall
" Allons Enfants ! "

A. MILES & CO. LTD., PRINTERS, 68-70, WARDOUR STREET, W.

PROGRAMME

Part 1
OVERTURE—" Fragments of French and Collisson."

PROLOGUE

"*Aut Chelsea aut Nullus*"—Origin of the name—Cæsar's commentary.
Potentates who have pervaded Chelsea—Henry VIII.; his method of house
hunting—Sir Thomas More, his "Happy Family."
Queen Elizabeth; supposed site of the historic mud puddle—Charles II.—
Song of the period : "Down by the Magpie and Stump."
The great men of yesterday : Turner, Carlyle and Sir Hans Sloane.
The rise and fall off of the Cremorne Gardens.
Whistler : his method—How to paint a nocturne in gold and silver.

Part 2
CHELSEA OF TO-DAY.
Some advertisements I have not been asked to show.
The boundaries of Chelsea, an artistic Colony.
" The Call of Cheyne Walk."
Some notable people, a selection from my photograph book.
Characteristics of Chelsea—The three ages of a soldier.
An American Lecturer on Chelsea and also on the French Revolution, showing
how Ward P. Dingus varied his lecture but not his lantern slides.
The song of the L.C.C. King.
The Chelsea of my dream.
The most beautiful view in Chelsea !

EPILOGUE

CONCERT GRAND BY BECHSTEIN,
Lantern Slides made by L. H. BAILEY, 33, Hasker Street, S.W.

The Twelve Pins

TO THE WEST

The Midland Great Western's doing its best,
And the circular ticket is safe in my vest;
But I feel that my holiday never begins
Till I'm in Connemara among the Twelve Pins.

The bank has no fortune of mine to invest
But there's money enough for the ones I love best;
All the gold that I want I shall find on the whins
When I'm in Connemara among the Twelve Pins.

Down by the Lough I shall wander once more,
Where the wavelets lap lap round the stones on the
shore;
And the mountainy goats will be wagging their chins
As they pull at the bracken among the Twelve Pins.

And it's welcome I'll be, for no longer I'll meet
The hard, pallid faces I find in the street;
The girl with blue eyes, and the boy with brown shins,
Will stand for their pictures among the Twelve Pins.

To-night, when all London's with gaslight agleam,
And the Carlton is filled with Society's cream,
I'll be 'takin' me tay' down at ould Johnny Flinn's
Safe an' away in the heart o' the Pins.

An' I've written my song, and it goes to the tune
Of The Mountains o' Mourne, so *colleen aroon*,
While I'm takin' me tay in this snuggest of inns,
Sing to me softly my song o' the Pins.

"THE RIVAL MAGICIANS."

SCENE. The Throne Room in the Palace of Dumdum, the
1st. King of Stoneybrokia.

(The King is discovered asleep on his
with filigree mitre round it, hung on
Pippip, his Page is asleep at his

Opening Chorus. (hear

Solo   We're going away for we ha
Chorus Yo, ho, let us go home,
Solo   Our wages we never shall
Chorus Give us our money and let

Chorus { Give us our due Dilly,
        { Give us our due,
        { Yo, ho, let us go home,
        { Think you might spare us
        { Give us our money and l

Solo   We're leaving him now wi
Solo   The poorest old Potenta
                        Repeat 5
        (As chorus dies away i
        rubs his eyes, and loo

Dum.   What ho! wake up there!

Pip.   (salaming) Here oh King!

Dum.   Where are the rest of you?

Pip.   You forget oh King, that they have not been paid their
        wages for ten years.

Dum.   (right elbow on knee, head on hand) "And therefore they
        desert me- (with sudden fury) Treacherous dogs: (Pippip jumps)
        Ah well (calming down) it is all for the best, they forfeit
        their salaries by this ignoble act- But you, good Pippip-
        you have not- (puts hand on Pippip's head) deserted me in
        mine hour of need.

Pip.   Oh no, oh King.

Drawing room theatricals were a feature of French family life.

*Back row: Hilda Marsh,
French, Hill Rowan,
Mollie, Ettie. Front:
Norah Muriel,
Enid Brown.*

33 CLIFTON HILL, N.W.
FRIDAY, APRIL 19th, 1907.

"The Rival Magicians"

(AN EPISODE IN THE LIFE OF
KING DUM-DUM THE WORST).

SCENE: The Throne Room in the Palace of Stoneybrokia.
TIME: See Clock.

Characters
(Good and otherwise).

Dum-Dum (A South-Eastern Potentate) ...	... HILL ROWAN (The Modern Garrick).
Lulu (His Daughter)	MOLLIE FRENCH (The Banjo Queen).
Pooh-Pooh (A romantic Prince)	ETTIE FRENCH (The Dramatic Wonder).
Bul-Bul (A Circassian Slave)	HILDA MARSH (Premier Danseuse).
Tut-Tut (Son of Yap-Yap)	ENID BROWN (The Tragic Marvel).
Pip-Pip (A Page)	NORAH MURIEL (From Daly's—specially engaged).
Yap-Yap (A Magician)	PERCY FRENCH (Specially disengaged).

ACCIDENTAL MUSIC BY MISS ALICE LINDÉ.

The Dances specially arranged by Miss HILDA MARSH and
Miss ENID BROWN.

Miss HILDA MARSH's and Miss MOLLIE FRENCH's Gowns by Madame
Alice Esty & Co.

Mr. PERCY FRENCH's Wardrobe by the Jumble Sale Dress Exchange.

DECEMBER, 1907.

Su. 1. 1st in Advent
M.   2.
Tu. 3.
W.   4.
Th. 5. *Chty. £9 & L'pool. Girls' Coll:*
F.   6.
Sa. 7. *Sandringham. Chty £10.10.*
Su. 8. 2nd in Advent
M.   9.
Tu. 10. *Mrs. Astley Roberts, Eastbourne c. aft. £5.*
W. 11. *Mrs. Shepherd. aft. Hove.*
Th. 12. *Miss Franks' School demons: Barrett" eng. per: "Bishop's Startf" aft. £*
Fr. 13. *Eastbourne*
Sa. 14. *Malvern College. Chty. £8.8. Children's Dancing demonstration.*
Su. 15. 3rd in Advent. *Mabel Day at home*
M. 16. *Clapham. Chty. £7.7. Miss J. Trent in mng. B. 9. ?*
Tu. 17. *Criterion mat: Wright Chty. "As you like it" with Ettie. mat. Whitcombe to*
W. 18. *Chigwell School. £5.5.   stay*
Th. 19. Full Moon O *Dine with the Milne's.*
F. 20.
Sa. 21. *Phyllis Water's party aft. Ettie. & Rowan's Children's party aft.*
Su. 22. 4th in Advent.
M. 23.
Tu. 24.
W. 25. (Christmas Day).
Th. 26. (Bank Holiday in England and Ireland)
F. 27.
Sa. 28. *Ashton £8.8. veans:*
Su. 29. 1st after Christmas.
M. 30. *Northampton. £8.8. com: to Chty. no. 1.*
Tu. 31.

PRETENDY LAND
SONG
words by
PERCY FRENCH
music by
J. A. Robertson.

Dedicated to my Cousin
CEDRIC COLLISSON

"MRS BRADY"
HUMOROUS
IRISH SONG
written by
PERCY FRENCH,
composed by
HOUSTON COLLISSON.

London.
JOSEPH WILLIAMS LIMITED,
32, Great Portland St. W.

PRICE 2/-

Percy French

My dear Mollie

It is hereditary in my family not to pass exams. So I look to you to Keep up the old family traditions. Your aunt Dora is rushing around at present attending lectures on various subjects at the British Associations, but as yet has only discovered that the very lowest race of savages live in New Guinea & not in Earls court as had been hitherto supposed. I met this boy behind this grin

at Greystones & he hoped you had not forgotten him.

This is a letter I began to write but lost it for a season.

Just been asked to Glenveigh for 21st ask Mummy if I can do this. am at present contemplating the cool & tranquil bogholes of Killucan

Your loving

Daddy

FRENCH, Percy, B.A., C.E.; Humourist, Artist, and Poet; b. 1854; 2nd s. of Christopher French, Cloonyquin, Co. Roscommon; m. 1st, 1890, Ethel Armytage Moore (d. 1891), of Arnmore, Co. Cavan; 2nd, 1894, Helen May Sheldon, of Burmington, Co. Warwick; three d. Educ.: Windermere College; Trinity College, Dublin. After College tried Civil Engineering for six years; editor of a Dublin humorous journal for two years; composed music and words of about thirty songs; took up Art, and painted some Irish scenes for the King; has united his talents in a combined song, story, and sketching entertainment; gave a series of recitals in London in 1899. Publications: The First Lord Liftinant, and other Stories; Phil the Fluter's Ball; and fifteen other humorous Irish songs; Noah's Ark, a fairy play produced at the Waldorf, 1905. Recreations: cycling, lawn tennis, water-colour sketching, and writing pathetic poems. Address: 48 Springfield Road, N.W. T.: 155, P.O. Hampstead. Club: Sesame.

Who's Who

STEINWAY HALL,
LOWER SEYMOUR STREET, W.

MR.

PERCY FRENCH

AT HOME

Thursday Afternoon,
May 7th, at 3.15.
(Under the Direction of Mr. L. G. SHARPE)

In a Series of New and Original Songs, Stories and Sketches in Colour.

NEW COSTUME I
NEW CHALK II
NEW PAPER III

L. G. SHARPE, CONCERT AGENCY,
44, REGENT STREET, LONDON, W.
Telephone No. 2164 Gerrard

PROGRAMME

Illustrated throughout with Rapid Sketches in Charcoal and Coloured Chalk.

PART I.

A SKETCH OF THE OLD IRISH DEER AND THE MORAL LESSON DEDUCED THEREFROM.

A FEW MORE NURSERY RHYMES
Rewritten by the Poets CHAUCER, SHELLEY, MOORE, HOOD and BURNS.

OUR ILLUSTRATED STORY—"BEAUTY AND THE BUNKER."

SOME SO-CALLED SONGS—
"GIRLS"—by a boy.   "THE DARLIN' GIRL FROM CLARE."

A NEW SCHOOL OF ART—
Showing how Illustrators can supply the Editors' outrageous demands for Summer landscapes in Winter, and Spring effects in Autumn.

"LIMERICKITIS."
A Terrible Tale of the Times.

FIVE MINUTES OF PROFOUND RELIEF.
(Only interrupted by a Rhyme and a Wriggle.)

PART II,

"HOW I WON THE OLYMPIC GAMES"
(A Tale of a great Grandfather.)

OUR BETTERS—THE BEASTS
"Now if you have likened a man to a beast,
In body, or feature, or brain,
The man's self esteem should be somewhat increased:
The beast is the one to complain."

MORE MINSTRELSY OF SORTS
"Snob's Society Guide."   "Chanson Français" (at least I think so.)

AN IDYLL OF THE SUBURBS
(Illustrated by my new Rotary Process.)

THE STORY OF THE MAN WHO FORGOT HE WAS DEAD.

AN IRISH NIGHT'S ENTERTAINMENT, concluding with THE PICTURE OF THE FEARSOME BEAST.

RED-LETTER DAYS

I was feeling slightly seedy
When a letter signed 'Mecredy'
Came across the Irish Channel to my home in London town;
And I said in language shoppy,
'Here's the Boss a wantin' copy,'
And my forehead corrugated in a formidable frown.

'Ho! Wagtale, wake from slumber!
For I want our Birthday Number
To contain a set of verses from thy venerable pate.
Send me something reminiscent
Of the days when first we listened
To thy songs around the campfire and we'll pay a special rate.'

It was not the extra rating
Sent these waves of thought vibrating
Through the years that lie behind me to the pre-pneumatic days,
When I rode a solid tyre,
And thought myself a flyer
If I beat the Allens' pony in a race to Ballyhaise.

But I always love to turn
To the feast of good St Hearn,
When with racquets on our handlebars we drank that day's delights;
How well our wheels would travel
O'er the Ballyhealy gravel,
How good those games of tennis! how grand our appetites!

I have still a fair digestion,
But could I - it's a question -
Eat plum pudding and play singles with these stalwart friends of mine,
Then home by moonlight fly it?
No, Jack Hearn! - let others try it,
You and I will fight those battles o'er the walnuts and the wine.

Then the day I went a-wheeling,
Round the lovely shores of Sheelin,
When the perfume of the Primrose told that spring had really come;
And I rode my cycle dreaming
That Beauty's eyes were beaming,
And I'd find cead mile failte in the halls of old Crossdrum!

Sweet Glen Finglas I'm your debtor,
For many a red letter
Must mark the days we cycled by Lough Katrine's silver strand.
Darrynane! thy sunset glory
I have painted con amore,
When she and I were members of Mecredy's merry band.

'Oh, my Tour-alluring laddie,'
I am now a white-haired daddy;
In an easy chair I'm sitting by a comfortable blaze,
But my thoughts away are winging
To the laughter and the singing
And the cycle bells a-ringing in those old red-letter days!

Ballyhaise, Ballyhealy, Lough Sheelin and Crossdrum are in County Cavan, Glen Finglas and Lough Katrine in Scotland, and Derrynane in County Kerry. Hearn was a cycling champion.

Glenveagh Castle was a favourite haunt of his. 'E.R.,' Edward Radcliffe, was a colleague from **The Jarvey** *days.*

TO E.R.

For you once heard the fairy bells,
And saw the little shehogues play,
And knew at last the magic spells
That lead the lover to Glenveagh.

Oh Poet, when the touch of Time
Has turned those auburn locks to grey,
Still may the bells of Faerie chime
That once re-echoed round Glenveagh.

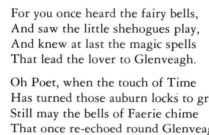

From the visitors' book.

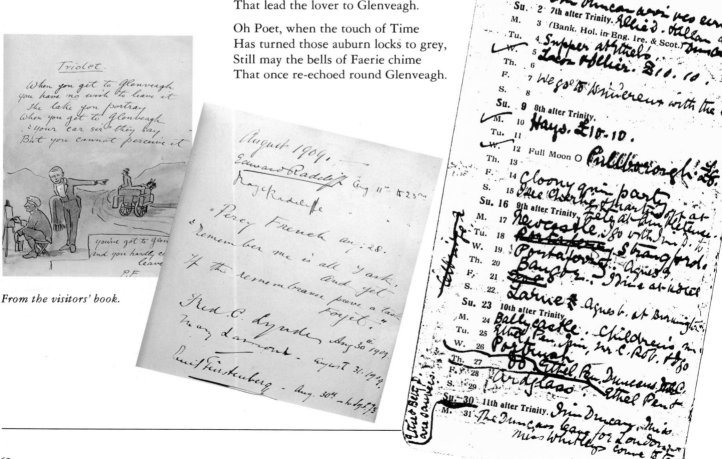

French loved painting more than anything else, and literally painted tens of thousands of watercolours. Sales of his paintings provided a useful income.

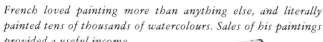

AUGUST, 1909.

Su. 1 8th after Trinity. Full Moon
M. 2 (Bank Hol. in Eng. Ire. & Scot.)
Tu. 3
W. 4
Th. 5
F. 6
S. 7
Su. 8 9th after Trinity.
M. 9
Tu. 10
W. 11 *Tramore. We come to Ireland.*
Th. 12
F. 13
S. 14
Su. 15 10th after Trinity
M. 16 *Newcastle*
Tu. 17 *Warren point*
W. 18
Th. 19 *Buncrana*
F. 20
S. 21 *Portstewart*
Su. 22 11th after Trinity
M. 23 *Portrush*
Tu. 24 *Ballycastle*
W. 25
Th. 26 *Rosapenna*
F. 27
S. 28 *Bundoran*
Su. 28 12th after Trinity.
M. 30 Full Moon
Tu. 31

An ould pagan of a dog

THE Painter and the Pianist
　　Were walking hand-in-hand,
"Suppose we try" the Painter said
"To give a one night stand
　　With me to write the dialogue,
　　And you to be the band!"

"Suppose we gave six Matinées"
　　Replied the Pianist,
"And cater for the young and old
　　In ways they can't resist."
"Do you suppose" the Painter said
　　"That we should both be hissed?"

"I doubt it," said the Pianist,
　　"I've always got recalls
And you have got a pretty wit,
　　A wit that never palls."
"We'll give a week" the Painter said,
　　"In Steinway's pillared Halls."

Now don't forget on Boxing Day,
　　From three to nearly five,
For just a week this merry pair
　　Will keep the game alive;
So on that day jump on a 'bus
　　And tell it where to drive.

And if the driver says he's got
　　To go to London Wall,
Or Parsons Green or Shepherd's Bush,
　　You answer "Not at all,
The only place that people go
　　This week is—Steinway Hall!"

Cut this out and present at New Dudley Gallery, 169, Piccadilly, and see Mr. Percy French's Water Colour Exhibition.

PROGRAMME
will include—

Overture　　　　"1910"　　　French and Collisson
MR. PERCY FRENCH AND DR. COLLISSON.

Mr. FRENCH
will then give the very latest phase of
"The oldest Joke in the World"
and afterwards give an imitation of himself
trying to sing a new and original ballad
"The long shore sailor man."

Dr. COLLISSON in his New NONSENSE SONGS.
(a).　　"The Infantile Tyrannical"
(b).　　"The Impotent Irascible"
(c).　　"The Frankly Homicidal"

Mr. FRENCH
will illustrate the Life of Napoleon I. and show
why he (Napoleon—not French) failed to
take London by storm.

Dr. COLLISSON
will relate his adventures at
"A Christmas Party."
Describing :—　　"Little Harry's SOLO"
"The Man who had a Joke"
"The Reciter"
and
"The Singer who hesitated"

DURING THE THREE MINUTES INTERVAL
The Painter and the Pianist will produce an
impromptu Poem Picture and Pianoforte Solo
from themes suggested by the audience.

Dr. COLLISSON
And the Pianoforte will give
"Jimmy's Christmas Eve"
written specially for him by JOHN SAVILE JUDD.

Mr. FRENCH
will do his best to entertain some small children, and,
if he survives, will sing
"The Oklahoma Rose"

Dr. COLLISSON
will (by request) sing one or two songs from the French- Collisson repertoire
"Mrs. Brady"　　"Donnegan's Daughter"　　"Golf"
"Maguire's Motor Bike"　　"Wait for a while now, Mary"
"Rafferty's Racin' Mare"　　"The Mountains o' Mourne"
"The Fortunes of Finnegan"　　"The Pride of Petravore"
"Are ye right there, Michael?"　　"Father O'Callaghan"

The Painter and Pianist will again combine to produce
"Our Panorama"
Lecturer and Scenic Artist　-　-　-　-　PERCY FRENCH.
Orchestra　-　-　-　-　-　-　HOUSTON COLLISSON.

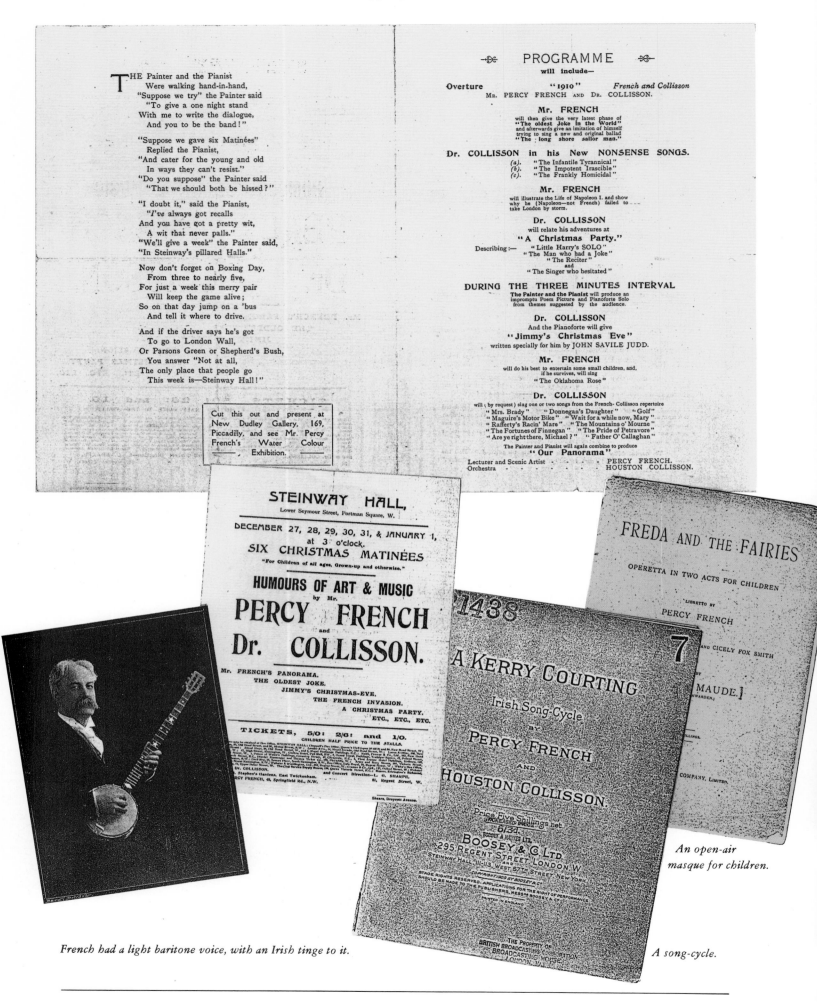

STEINWAY HALL,
Lower Seymour Street, Portman Square, W.

DECEMBER 27, 28, 29, 30, 31, & JANUARY 1,
at 3 o'clock.

SIX CHRISTMAS MATINÉES
"For Children of all ages, Grown-up and otherwise."

HUMOURS OF ART & MUSIC
by Mr.
PERCY FRENCH
and
Dr. COLLISSON.

Mr. FRENCH'S PANORAMA.
THE OLDEST JOKE.
JIMMY'S CHRISTMAS-EVE.
THE FRENCH INVASION.
A CHRISTMAS PARTY.
ETC., ETC., ETC.

TICKETS, 5/0: 2/6: and 1/0.
CHILDREN HALF PRICE TO THE STALLS.

1438
A KERRY COURTING
Irish Song-Cycle
by
PERCY FRENCH
AND
HOUSTON COLLISSON.

Price Five Shilling net.
6/3d.
BOOSEY & C°. LTD.
295 REGENT STREET LONDON W

FREDA AND THE FAIRIES
OPERETTA IN TWO ACTS FOR CHILDREN

LIBRETTO BY
PERCY FRENCH
AND CICELY FOX SMITH

MAUDE.]

COMPANY, LIMITED.

French had a light baritone voice, with an Irish tinge to it.

A song-cycle.

An open-air masque for children.

THE FOUR FARRELLYS

In a small hotel in London I was sitting down to dine
When the waiter brought the register and asked me if I'd sign.
And as I signed I saw a name that set my heart astir –
A certain Francis Farrelly had signed the register.
I knew a lot of Farrellys and out of all the crew
I kept on 'sort of wonderin' which Farrelly were you.
And when I'd finished dinner I sat back in my chair
Going round my native land to find what Farrelly you were.

South

Where you the keen-eyed Kerryman I met below Kenmare,
Who told me that when Ireland fought 'the odds were never fair.'
If Cromwell had met Sarsfield or met Owen Roe O'Neill,
It's not to Misther Gladstone we'd be lookin' for repeal.
Would have Ireland for the Irish, not a Saxon to be seen,
And only Gaelic spoken in that House in College Green.
Told me landlords wor the Divil! their agints tin times worse,
And iv'ry sort of governmint for Ireland was a curse!
Oh! if you're that Francis Farrelly your dreams have not come true
Still, Slainthe! Slainthe! Fransheen, for I like a man like you!

North

Or were you the Francis Farrelly that often used to say
He'd like to blow them Papishes from Darry walls away,
The boy who used to bother me that Orange Lodge to join
And thought that history started with the Battle o' the Boyne –
I was not all with ye, Francis, the Pope is not ma friend,
But still I hope poor man he'll die without that bloody end –
And when yer quit from care yerself and get to Kingdom Come,
It's no use teachin' you the harp – you'll play the Orange drum!
Och! man, ye wor a fighter, of that I had no doubt
For I seen ye in Belfast one night when the Antrim Road was out!
And many a time that evinin' I thought that ye wor dead,
The way them Papish pavin' stones was hoppin' off yer head.
Oh if you're the Francis Farrelly who came from North Tyrone
Here's lookin' to ye Francis but do leave the Pope alone.

East

Or were you the Francis Farrelly that in my college days
For strolling on the Kingstown Pier had such a curious craze.
D'ye mind them lovely sisters – the blonde and the brunette,
I know I've not forgotten and I don't think you forget!
That picnic at the Dargle – and th'other at the Scalp,
How my heart was palpitatin' – but hers wasn't – not a palp!
Someone said ye married money – and maybe ye were wise,
But the gold you loved was in her hair and the di'monds in her eyes.
So I like to think ye married her and that you're with her yet,
'Twas some 'meleesha' officer that married the brunette,
But the blonde one always loved ye and I knew you loved her too,
So me blessin's on ye Francis and the blue sky over you.

West

Or were you the Francis Farrelly I met so long ago
In the bogs below Belmullet, in the County of Mayo.
That long-legged freckled Francis with the deep-set wistful eyes
That seem to take their colour from those ever changing skies
That put his flute together as I sketched the distant scene
And played me 'Planxty Kelly' and the 'Wakes of Inniskeen.'
That told me in the autumn he'd be sailin' to the west
To try and make his fortune and send money to the rest.
And would I draw a picture of the place where he was born
That out there when he looked at it he'd not feel so forlorn.
And when I had it finished you got up from where you sat
And you said 'Well you're the Divil and I can't say more than that.'
Oh if you're that Francis Farrelly your fortune may be small,
But I'm thinking – thinking – Francis that I love you best of all,
And I never can forget you – though it's years and years ago –
In the bogs below Belmullet, in the County of Mayo.

MR. FRENCH who is well known in artistic circles as a landscape painter as well as a humourist has added a serious lecture on drawing and painting to his programmes. As MR. FRENCH begins and finishes a large coloured picture on the platform and gives numerous examples in black and white, this lecture is entertaining as well as instructive.

THE LECTURE IS ENTITLED—

"Why don't we all Draw."

SYNOPSIS.—Why don't we all Draw—The danger of preconceived Ideas, the Simplicity of the Unknown—The one Rule in Perspective and how to apply it—The Choice of a Subject, where to Begin—Values, Light and Shade—Composition.

The Primary Colours, how to tell the right Blue, Yellow and Red—The best Proportions—the Magic of Grey—The Sky—The highest Light—The Distance—The middle Distance—The Foreground—The deepest Dark—The Result!

MR. FRENCH can also entertain a drawing room party by producing really beautiful pictures on a plate, by means of candle smoke and a match. The above sketch of Kings Road, Chelsea, is a specimen of this wonderful art. The plate can be varnished and preserved.

The Public Schools on Mr. Percy French.

Rev. Dr. JAMES, Head Master of Rugby, writes:
 "We were greatly delighted with your entertainment, the second programme was quite as good as the first."

Rev. Dr. J. WOOD, Head Master of Harrow, writes:
 "Excellent!—quite irresistibly funny, with just the right sort of fun."

Rev. Dr. WAY, Head Master of Rossall, writes
 "Delighted with your entertainment. It was in perfect taste, and remarkable for its originality and humour,"

C. MORRIS, Esq., M.A., Head Master of the South Eastern College, Ramsgate, writes:
 "Mr. French is the best man we have ever had.—For Schools he is a real find."

The Principal of the London School for Girls, writes:
 "A delightful entertainment—we have never spent such an enjoyable evening."

Mr. French has also performed several times and wtih great success at Marlborough, Wellington, H Repton, Tonbridge, Clongowes, Castleknock, Fettes, Glenalmond, and many other Schools.

 * A selection of Mr. French's water Colours can be seen at the modern Gallery, 61, New Bond Street.

VAIL AND CO., 170, FARRINGDON F

In July the Frenches moved back to Clifton Hill, to No. 27.

CHAPTER FIVE:

'ACROSS THE ATLANTICAL SEA'

New York fr the Hudson.   Percy French

Dear Danny,
I'm takin' the pen in me hand
To tell you we're just out o' sight o' the land;
In the grand Allan liner we're sailin' in style,
But we're sailin' away from the Emerald Isle;
And a long sort o' sigh seemed to rise from us all
As the waves hid the last bit of ould Donegal.
Och! it's well to be you that is takin' yer tay
Where they're cuttin' the corn in Creeshla the day.

The North American tour of 1910. After a send-off at Paddington Station, French, aged 56, and Collisson, aged 45, left from Southampton on Michaelmas Day, 29th September.

Cartoon by Ernest Mills.

Two Clever Entertainers.

COMING over on the Royal Edward to undertake their American engagements, including the Massey Hall entertainment on Wednesday evening, Mr. Percy French and Houston Collison, Mus. Doc., were exceedingly popular passengers. They both assisted at the concert on the ship, and on several evenings in the lounge made things lively in their own refined Irish way. Mr. French made several warm friends through his story of how a friend of his tried to tell a story at a children's party. So delightful was the impression he conveyed of an unruly mob of children interrupting with question and the frantic efforts of his friend to satisfy their demands for information and to finish his story at the same time, that the white haired Irishman was lugged off to the smoking room by his admirers, among whom were some of the returning Canadian and American writers, where he sat as in the sketch above telling yarns that seemed to grow better and better as the good ship plowed through the miles of gray Atlantic night on her way to the Belle Isle Straits.

At the ship's concert, Mr. French had a curious experience. One of the stewards, who is something of a comedian, was on the programme. His offering turned out to be one of French's own rollicking Irish songs; whether the rendering of the words and the musical accompaniment were to his liking was not entirely apparent, but those who were near him say the brilliant Irishman's face was a study.

SEPTEMBER 1910.

THUR. 1.
FRI. 2.
SAT. 3.
Sun. 4 15th after Trinity.
MON. 5.
TUES. 6.
WED. 7.
THUR. 8.
FRI. 9.
SAT. 10.
Sun. 11 16th after Trinity.
MON. 12.
TUES. 13.
WED. 14.
THUR. 15.
FRI. 16.
SAT. 17.
Sun. 18 17th after Trinity
MON. 19. O Full Moon.
TUES. 20.
WED. 21.
THUR. 22.
FRI. 23.
SAT. 24.
Sun. 25 18th after Trinity.
MON. 26.
TUES. 27.
WED. 28.
THUR. 29. Michaelmas Day.
FRI. 30.

The words of two songs were written on board ship. **The Emigrant's Letter** was inspired by a remark heard on board: 'Well then, Mick, they'll be cuttin' the corn in Creeshlough the day.' Ernest Hastings wrote the music.

The family in London reading one of French's letters from America. They had this photograph taken and sent out to him for Christmas. From left: Mollie, Ettie, Lennie, Joan.

In Canada.

My dear family, the gallery of fair females arrived on Christmas Eve, so, in the words of Francis Farrelly, 'I could hang them up to look at them and not feel so forlorn.'

(from New York).

Boston

HOTEL WESTMINSTER
BOSTON, MASSACHUSETTS
C. A. GLEASON

To Ettie (nov. 4. 1910)

I've wandered round Toronto
I've wandered round Quebec
Yet can't find what I want to
See hanging round your neck

I saw some pretty trinkets
Some jewels that might do
But always said "I think its
not good enough for you".

I've searched in Boston city
I've searched in Montreal
And the burden of my ditty
Is — there's nothing there at all

Its really most distressing
My search has been in vain
So I'm sending you my blessing
and these fancies from my brain

They will fly across the water
To the home in Clifton Hill
and tell my dear dear daughter
That I'm thinking of her still.

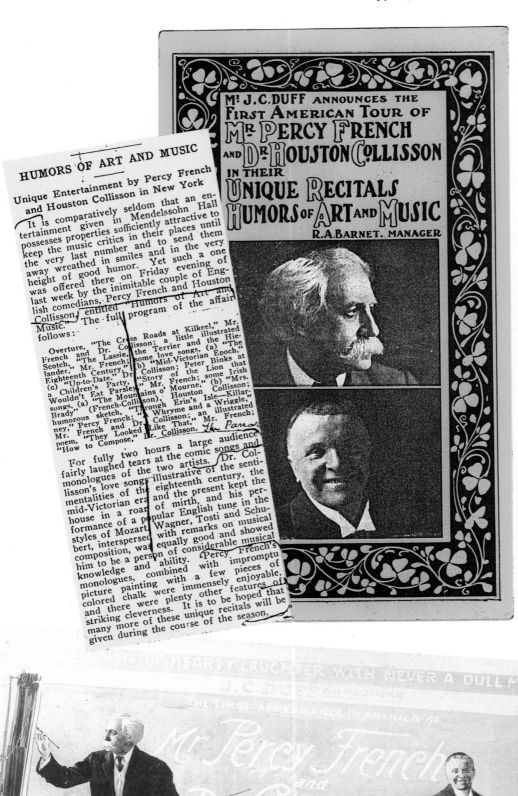

HUMORS OF ART AND MUSIC

Unique Entertainment by Percy French and Houston Collison in New York

It is comparatively seldom that an entertainment given in Mendelssohn Hall possesses properties sufficiently attractive to keep the music critics in their places until the very last number and to send them away wreathed in smiles and in the very height of good humor. Yet such a one was offered there on Friday evening of last week by the inimitable couple of English comedians, Percy French and Houston Collison, entitled "Humors of Art and Music." The full program of the affair follows:

Overture, "The Cross Roads at Kilkeel," Mr. French and Dr. Collisson; a little illustrated Scotch, "The Lassie, the Terrier and the Hielander," Mr. French; some love songs, (a) "The Eighteenth Century," (b) "Mid-Victorian Epoch," (c) "Up-to-Date," Dr. Collisson; Peter Binks at a Children's Party, Mr. French; some Irish songs, (a) "The Mountains o' Mourne," (b) "Mrs. Brady," (French-Collison) Houston Collisson; humorous sketch, "Through Erin's Isle—Killarney," Percy French; "Whryme and a Wriggle," Mr. French and Dr. Collisson; an illustrated poem, "They Looked Like That," Mr. French; "How to Compose," Dr. Collisson, the Piano.

For fully two hours a large audience fairly laughed tears at the comic songs and monologues of the two artists. Dr. Collisson's love songs, illustrative of the sentimentalities of the eighteenth century, the mid-Victorian era and the present kept the house in a roar of mirth, and his performance of a popular English tune in the styles of Mozart, Wagner, Tosti and Schubert, interspersed with remarks on musical composition, was equally good and showed him to be a person of considerable musical knowledge and ability. Percy French's impromptu monologues, combined with a few pieces of picture painting with colored chalk were immensely enjoyable, and there were plenty other features of striking cleverness. It is to be hoped that many more of these unique recitals will be given during the course of the season.

Mr. J. C. DUFF ANNOUNCES THE FIRST AMERICAN TOUR OF Mr. PERCY FRENCH AND Dr. HOUSTON COLLISSON IN THEIR UNIQUE RECITALS HUMORS OF ART AND MUSIC
R. A. BARNET, MANAGER

TWAIN AND CARUSO REVISED.

French and Collisson in Boston with Pocket Edition Entertainment.

"He," began the man who wore his brown hair in a bang, indicating the man who wore his white hair long and rumpled, "is the unabridged sketcher-writer-reader — unabridged because so tall."

"He," continued the man who wore his white hair long and rumpled, indicating the man who wore his brown hair in a bang, "is the pocket-edition tenor — pocket edition because so short. He can write music."

"And he," said the tenor, whose name is Dr. Houston Collisson, "thinks he looks like Mark Twain."

"And he," added the unabridged, whose name is Percy French and who really does look like Mark Twain, "thinks he sounds like Caruso."

"We're both Irish," they volunteered, "and many of our songs and stories are Irish, not burlesque, stage Irish, but real Irish. We never were in the States till last week. We want to see a football game and an Indian." They glanced round the lobby of the Hotel Westminster as if either sight might appear at any moment.

But they acted like that only because they are funny. Theirs, in fact, is a funny business. Dr. Collisson, the short, stout, red-faced man, writes funny music—good music, of course, but the kind that makes people laugh. And he sings funny songs in a funny way. Also, he impersonates noted musical people. "For instance," he explained, "we were giving an entertainment in London, and I impersonated Sig. Tosti. All of a sudden I saw the people turning round and whispering, and I didn't know what was the trouble. When I finished, who should rise up in his seat but Tosti himself. 'Thank you!' he shouted, bowing; 'very kind! Many thanks! Not a bit angry.'"

"Underneath," interrupted Mr. French seriously "underneath the humorist in Dr. Collisson, there is the truly excellent musician." Dr. Collisson squirmed. "He is a doctor of music in Dublin University. Most people take me for the doctor, because I look like a dignified family physician. Dr. Collisson has written some operettas and some high class music. He's very well known in England and abroad."

"Yes," reflected Dr. Collisson, "not so many years ago I wouldn't have anything to do with music unless it was classic. I played at symphonies and such things, and conducted them, and I wouldn't have my name on a program if there was a bit of humorous music there. But now I've acquired common sense."

There came a pause. Mr. French looked meaningly at Dr. Collisson. Dr. Collisson looked aimlessly at the rug. "Well," said Mr. French, "native modesty forbids my telling about myself. I've told about you, but if you won't tell about me, I suppose I'll have to fling aside all natural reticence."

"Oh!" said Dr. Collisson, "of course. Why, you see, Mr. French writes most amusing verses and stories, and reads them in a most amusing way. Then he talks in an amusing way, and as he tells the story he draws illustrative pictures in colors on big sheets of paper. They're extremely entertaining pictures. But under the humorous sketcher there is the real artist. Mr. French has a wide reputation as a painter of fine water colors. And—and—well, here's a pamphlet telling all about us."

"Not all," corrected Mr. French, "but almost."

"Mr. French's biography, of course, is very largely expurgated," said the doctor of music, "but my deeds are down there in full. I haven't any past—yet."

The pamphlet substantiated both narratives, and furnished the further information that when, at the age of 19, Mr. Collisson became a doctor of music, he was the youngest doctor of music in the world, and that several of Mr. French's water colors were in the galleries of the late King and of the Marchioness of Londonderry. The composer-singer-pianist and the author-reader-artist said they were to give an entertainment in Jordan Hall on the evening of Nov. 2, and were induced to admit that it would probably be a very fine entertainment. As proof, they told how, after they had given entertainments in London, the Savages and the Irish Club dined them, and a crowd of 1500, plus a brass band, playing "Come Back to Erin," escorted them to Paddington station.

"You'd better come to hear us and see the pictures," they concluded, "for we're going to be awfully funny."

French and Collisson returned home via the West Indies.

OFF TO THE WEST INDIES

Dear ones in my happy home
We are sailing o'er the foam
Anchor tripped and helm a-lee
(Not quite sure what that may be)
For the Caribbean Sea!

Doctor looking rather pale
Prospect of a six-days' sail!
Only fancy, we shall glide,
Where the wild Bahamas ride.

What they ride I never knew,
Will know it in a day or two -
Live on flying fish and fruits,
Empty scorpions from our boots!

Mounted on a trusty steed,
Chase the deadly centipede,
Beard the beetle in his den,
'On a peak of Darien.',

Then with faces wreathed in smiles
Turning from the Windward Isles,
Sail across the wobbling main
Till we reach our homes again.

'Off to the West Indies'

Trinidad, West Indies

RAFTING DOWN THE RIO

Come sit beside the fire, old friend,
And dream that bamboo stems
Have risen up around us
'Mid flowers that shine like gems.
And we are back in fairyland,
And thro' the golden haze
We're rafting down the Rio
In the old Jamaica days.

Oh the old Jamaica days!
Faintly through that leafy maze
Comes the croon of Creole melodies
As down the stream one strays
Till the fireflies sparkle round us
In those darkened waterways
And we're rafting down the Rio
In the old Jamaica days.

In those mighty mountain ranges
What memories lie hid,
Through the stricken streets of Kingston
Stalks the ghost of Captain Kidd.
While a phantom Henry Morgan
Sets Port Royal in a blaze
As we're rafting down the Rio
In the old Jamaica days.

Oh the old Jamaica days!
How we used to lie and laze
And think of people working
As a curious kind of craze,
Wear and tear of brain and muscle
How we wondered if it pays
As we rafted down the Rio
In the old Jamaica days.

There's a terror in the treetops
And where the shadows brood
For the wild cat and the scorpion
And the snakes are seeking food.
The alligators blink at us
From fever-haunted bays
And the woods knew Devil worship
In those old Jamaica days.

Oh the old Jamaica days!
When the sun's mid-winter rays
Have failed to pierce the fogs that fill
Our murky alleyways.
We'll sit beside the fire, old friend,
And as the embers blaze
Go rafting down the Rio
In the old Jamaica days.

French and Collinson arrived back home on Easter Monday, 1911.

THE FRENCH-COLLISSON MATINEES.

Mr. Percy French and Dr. Houston Collisson, who have just returned from a tour of America, where they gained much favour, are making merry at the Steinway Hall every afternoon this week. Their programme is almost, if not entirely, new, and many of the sketches have a connection with their American experiences. Among these is the Grand Panorama of America, in which Mr. Percy French, besides lecturing in a light and humorous manner, does many wonderful drawings in chalk, while Dr. Collisson, at the pianoforte, occasionally interpolates a song. Another good piece of fun is Dr. Collisson's sketch "How I Became a Successful Vocalist in America," in which he expounds the art of suiting your song to your audience. Mr. French has brought away an amusing impression of a Broadway book-auctioneer, whose learning is more various than correct. There is a new Irish song dealing with "Flanagan's Flying Machine," and a very entertaining satire on a suburban "at home" day. Mr. French also discourses on the Post-Impressionists, remarking that, according to that school, the best way to produce a good figure picture is to start it as a landscape. To make his point clear Mr. French transforms a chalk drawing of an Irish sunrise into a full-length portrait of a girl. The two popular artists are excellent company, and their entertainment is as amusing as it is unique.

STEINWAY HALL.

An excellent entertainment of light drawing-room humour is furnished this week in the Steinway Hall by Mr. Percy French and Dr. Collisson, after their tour in the New World. These two talented artists have drawn up a programme full of interest and variety, and they contrive to keep the attention of the auditor continually on the alert as to what they are going to do next. Dr. Collisson's specialities are the voice and pianoforte, while his colleague is an adept with the crayons, and these gifts are turned to good account in the various sketches that make up the bill. The best of the songs are undoubtedly the topical "Flanagan's Flying Machine" and "In London Town," where witty texts have been set to apt, insinuating melodies. Indeed, the tune of the first one, with its light-hearted lilt, immediately sets the heart agog, and purses up the whistler's lips. It is little things like these that keep alive the sensation of perennial youth. To single out examples from Mr. French's impromptu drawings where all reach the same expert level is not easy, but those representing scenes in America met with great success. As regards the sketches themselves, Dr. Collisson, representing "Mrs. Balham-Tooting" receiving her guests at an "At Home," and Mr. French, impersonating a Broadway bookseller disposing of his stock by auction, kept the audience in a continual state of merriment. In his "Illustrated Sketch," entitled "A Post Impression," Mr. French recited a serious narrative poem in a dignified, impressive manner, drawing busily all the time, and a peculiar piquancy of suspense was imparted to the story by the disconnected, desultory manner of recitation due to his simultaneous occupation with the crayon. An effective climax was then reached when the finished picture was turned upside down, and proved to be another one in close connection with the poem. Mention must also be made of the new game of "Double Squiggles," which was played with the audience, and caused unbounded delight. It is good to have entertainers like these among us to keep alive the laughter of the world.

Photograph by the fashionable Edwardian photographer Ernest Mills.

Has anybody ever been to Mick's Hotel,
Mick's Hotel by the salt say water?
None o'yez ha' been there – just as well!
Just as well for ye! – Oh!
If ye were an ostheridge ye might contrive
To get away from the place alive;
They charge you a dollar for a meal you couldn't swaller,
And it's down by the silver sea.

THE TOUCAN

A most unwieldy sort of bill
Is owned by every Toucan;
I cannot tell what want they fill -
I only hope that *you* can!

THE CONDOR

This creature loves to close his eyes,
And on his past to ponder;
He thinks it makes him look quite wise -
It doesn't, Mr. Condor!

THE SECRETARY BIRD

The Secretary (cocks and hens)
A useful bird appears
And carries quite a lot of pens
Behind his ears.

THE PORPOISE

The Porpoise jumps - when so inclined -
The rope with which they warp us.
It has a very active mind
And very active corpus.
But in these jumps I fail to find
The purpose of the porpoise!

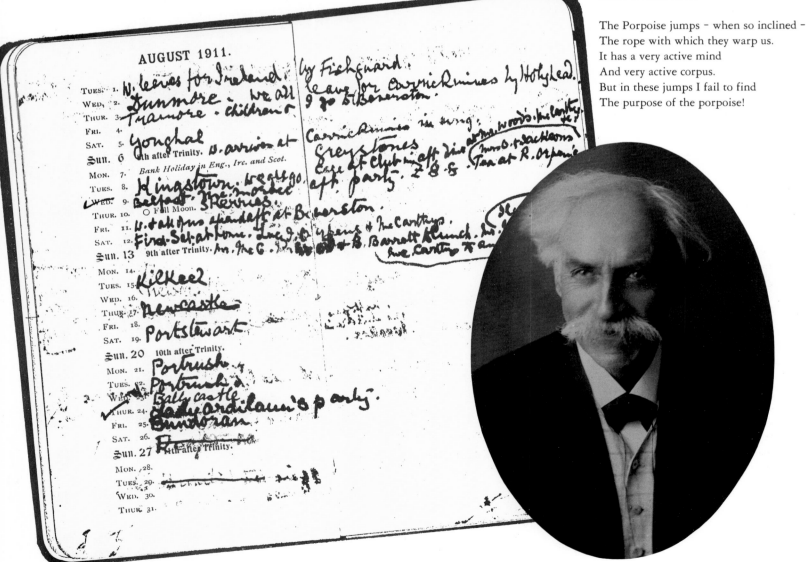

TWO NEW "FRENCH" SONGS.

A song by that racy Irish balladist and composer Mr. Percy French is always sure of a hearty welcome; two songs by him are doubly welcome. The "French" style is quite in a class by itself and has set a standard all its own. In comics he is of the broad and witty type where the words trip merrily along and the laugh soon follows: in serio-humorous or sentimental songs he blends a tuneful verse with a hauntingly pleasing pathos, simple and tenderly touching.

The two latest "French" songs are certain to be well received and heard soon in concerts and "smokers." "Mick's Hotel" is a merry comic number with a catchy refrain; the other song is of the quasi-humorous kind, half sad half sorrowful.

"Mick's Hotel," words and music by Percy French; "The Emigrant's Letter, or Cutting the Corn," words by Percy French, music by Ernest Hastings. (Dublin: Pigott and Co. 2s net each).

Ode to Joan.

The sun may shine
From ten to nine
along the brine-
-y way
The swine may dine
on turpentine
and with good wine
be gay

The Porcupine
with prickley spine
with fine young Kine
may play

This was a blot,
but
now it's not

no 'friend of mine'
need weep or whine
For Joan is mine
To day!

With Lennie.

Music by Ettie.

Come back, Paddy Reilly, to Ballyjamesduff,
Come home, Paddy Reilly, to me.

Paddie Reilly was the local jarvey at Ballyjamesduff. French went there one year only to learn that he had emigrated.

French was a great favourite as an entertainer at the public schools.

Sketch by Kitty Lloyd.

THE MUSICIAN TO HIS LOVE

Sing me no song to charm the twilight hour!
Your nerve is strong but mine's a fragile flower.
Sing when I'm far from here, say in Hong Kong,
But, if you love me, dear, sing me no sing.

When I the prelude played, and bade you sing,
Oh! the strange noise we made! The jangling!
White notes I found were wrong, so were the black,
For you had pitched the song right in the crack!

If thou wert dumb and not a single note
Could ever come from out that rounded throat,
My love I'd tell on finger and on thumb,
Oh, I could love thee well if thou wert dumb!

If I were deaf I'd love to let thee sing
In C or F, and watch thy guests take wing;
I'd see thee shriek and yell above the treble clef,
Thou couldst not break the spell if I were deaf!

You have no ear – no ear for tune or rhyme,
And, it is very clear, no sense of time.
Sing to my wealthy aunt, her nerves are strong,
But, if it's me you want – sing me no song!

Ettie set this to music.

PERCY FRENCH AT CHRIST'S HOSPITAL, HORSHAM

In the introductory patter French imagined himself to be the unfortunate man who had been appointed artist and poet on the staff of a monthly magazine. He had just been told one January morning that material for the summer number must be prepared well in advance, in fact at once. On this wintry day he gazed out of the window and seeing nothing but falling snow murmured dismally: 'How can I write a poem about summer? All I can think of is:

> The snow, the snow!
> Where does it come from?
> Where does it go?
> I'm an ignorant man,
> So I don't know.'

Despairingly he thought of the cover design he had to produce and turned to his easel on which was mounted an outsize tear-off drawing block. As he was apparently doodling, a picture appeared of pine trees in a snowy landscape with strong shadows in the moonlight. As he stood back to look at this effort he remarked gloomily 'That doesn't look much like summer to me. Let's see what it looks like upside down.' Suiting the action to the word he turned the drawing block and revealed a picture of a little fleet of sailing boats coming into harbour on a beautiful summer evening.

(Arthur Killingley)

Prince of our entertainers, best loved, was Percy French. Old now and frail, with a mane of white hair and a drooping moustache, he insisted on arriving early and having tea in the School House with the boys. Those lucky enough to be at the chosen table would be entertained with all manner of stories, card tricks, and strange beasts made from napkins and newspaper. Two or three would receive landscapes executed in candle-smoke on plate or saucer, and fixed with a kind of varnish, which they would gladly purchase from the school and treasure in their studies. Then, his vitality heightened, the old man would mount the platform in the gym, and give the most versatile single entertainment I have seen from anyone but Danny Kaye. He would sing in a sweet small tenor voice, accompanying himself on the guitar. He would paint a landscape on a large sheet of paper draped over a blackboard, telling stories all the time, then turn it upside down and reveal it as something entirely different. The applause commanded by Percy French rang louder and longer than anyone else's; and I, who had heard him also in Ireland, felt a thrill of national pride.

(L.A.G. Strong, Brighton College)

CHELSEA PALACE

KING'S ROAD, S.W.

TWICE NIGHTLY
At 6.30 and 9.
Monday, August 12th, 1912.
AND DURING THE WEEK.
The same Artistes appear at both performances.

First Production of a New Musical Fantasy
entitled :

A FROG HE WOULD

Book by Percy French.
Music by A. J. Robertson.

Cast :

The Frog	- -	Mr. IVAN BERLYN
The Mouse	- -	Miss ANNIE HEENAN
The Mother Frog	-	Miss MARY HAY
The Lily-white Duck	-	Miss MAY FOSTER
Anthony Rowley	-	Mr. BRENDON STEWART
The Rat	- -	Mr. SAM WALSH

Chorus of Moths and Butterflies

BELLE DAVIS

AND HER CRACKER JACKS

In

"SOUTHERN PASTIMES"

PALACE BIOSCOPE
Showing Latest Pictures

FRED POPLAR
Comedian.

FOOT-GERS

Anglo-French Comedian and Mimic

GULLIVER

1d. PROGRAMME 1d.
Monday, Aug. 12th, 1912, at 6.40 & 9.10.

SPECIAL NOTICE.—At the commencement of each performance a series of Novel & Interesting Pictures will be shown by The World's Advertising Co., 11 Old Jewry Chambers, E.C.

1 Overture "La Petite Armée" *Marchetti*
2 Gulliver and the Doll with the laugh, in a Comedy Ventriloquial Act
3 Fred Poplar, *Comedian*
4 The Romps, *In an Entree of Mirth*
5 Duprez & Fibre, *American Vaudeville Artistes*
6 Kitty Wager, *Comedienne*
7 Doody & Wright, *In a striking Comedy Act*
8 Foot-Gers, *Anglo French Comedian and Mimic*
9 Selection, "Let me Whisper" *Donaldson*
10 Belle Davis and her Cracker Jacks, in Southern Pastimes
11 R. H. Douglass, *In his latest sketch, "Types from Stageland."*
12 First Production of a new Musical Fantasy
    "A FROG HE WOULD."
    Book by Percy French
    The Frog..Ivan Berlyn
    The Mouse..Annie Heenan
    The Mother Frog..Mary Hay
    Music by J. A. Robertson.
    The Lily-White Duck..May Foster
    Anthony Rowley..Brendan Stewart
    THE RAT..SAM WALSH
    Chorus of Moths and Butterflies
    Scene—A Street in Paris—Night.
    Produced by Brendan Stewert
    Dresses designed by Gwendoline Butler.
13 Palace Pictures, *Showing latest Films*
14 March - "The President" *Swasta*

1912.

INNISMEELA

I can only see the moonbeam that on Innismeela floats,
But if I slept inside the fairies' ring,
I'd see them sailing, sailing, in their little silver boats,
And I'd hear the songs the Little People sing.
For the Fairy-Man has told me of what happened there one day,
When he woke to find them dancing on the shore,
And still he hears them singing, though 'tis faint and far away,
And he's wishing he was with them evermore.

I've seen the Queen of Fairyland! I've heard her wondrous song,
With her to heights of happiness I've flown,
Now I know the days are weary, now I know the nights are long,
For the one I love has left me all alone.
Innismeela! Innismeela! there's a sleep that knows no dream,
And it's in that dreamless slumber I shall be,
For I know that I shall waken by some still celestial stream
And through the golden light she'll come to me.

At a banquet held on 4th January at Dublin's Gresham Hotel to celebrate the silver wedding of R. J. Mecredy, editor of the Irish Cyclist and Motor Cyclist, French read these lines.

WHEN FIRST I KNEW MECREDY

When first I knew Mecredy
We were rather poor and needy
(Take this *cum grano salis,* for a poet must have rhymes)
What I mean is that Dame Fortune
Took longer to importune,
And men made money slowly in those pre-pneumatic times.

I had failed at engineering,
When a letter, rather cheering,
Came to tell me I was wanted on the old I.C. and A.,
And I saw my verses printed –
The type was small, I hinted,
But still I think the type was rather larger than the pay.

How we used to plan the ruin
Of that rival rag, the 'Blue 'un,'
At its make-up and its matter we kept turning up our nose;
And we wondered who could read it,
We ourselves had not succeeded
In wading through its piffle – how we hated the du Cros!

How we slanged E. J. O'Reilly –
Whom we think of now so highly –
How furious the battle of the 'Yallers' and the 'Blues.'
Oh, we pilloried and bled 'em,
Though Harvey, senior, led 'em,
But this is ancient history – before the MOTOR NEWS.

Other times brought other manners;
Soon beneath Dunlopian banners
We joined our former foemen with hearts devoid of care,
And we found that Harvey really
Was a man we liked sincerely –
It's hard to keep on sneering at a multi-millionaire.

But I'm straying from my topic –
'Arjay' the Philanthropic,
What he's done for Irish cyclists makes him worthy of the name.
If *I* had worked as *he* did,
I, too, might have succeeded,
And be sitting there sedately while another sang my fame.

Some people may not know it,
But the painter and the poet
Were included in his 'make up' when Mecredy went to press.
I have known him grow quite gushing,
O'er the day-dawn faintly flushing
The Connemara mountains and the river at Recess.

It is now an ancient story
How 'Arjay' would ride to glory,
And no matter what the race was would have something up his sleeve.
And when beaten, boiled, bedraggled,
His curly head he waggled,
And 'pipped' the would-be winner without by or with your leave.

And when my children's children,
Come round me with bewilderin'
Requests for some true story, I will scratch mine ancient pate,
And tell how Gatehouse looked, lads,
When he knew 'Arjay' was cooked, lads,
And suddenly those spectacles came flashing down the straight.

So here's R. J. Mecredy,
The spectacled, the speedy,
His racing days are over, but we meet to-night to show,
By the way in which we fete him,
And with this plate donate him,
We still appreciate him as we did long years ago!

IF you ask me, oh my children
  Whence this legend and tradition,
  Whence this most astounding story,
Whence this tale of tennis playing ;
I would answer, I would tell you :
It was written by a poet,
By a poor but pleasant poet,
Who supports an aged landlord,
And a flock of hungry tradesmen,
Not to mention tax collectors,
Gas and water-rate collectors,
Who keep dancing on his doorstep.

So in his suburban attic
He must grind out comic copy !
With his comrade, Hubert Leslie,
Working at the illustrations,
Till their book is on the market,
Selling by the hundred thousand ;
Then the vultures are contented
—For the time they are contented—
And the wolves forego their howling
—For a time forego their howling.

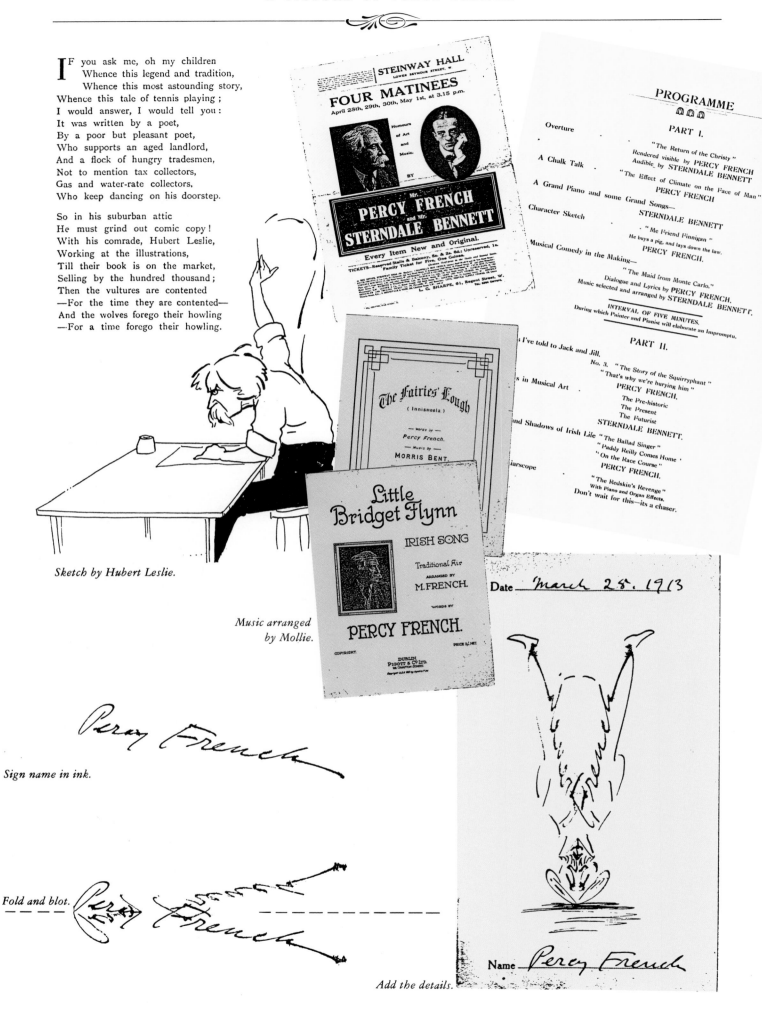

Sketch by Hubert Leslie.

*Music arranged
by Mollie.*

Sign name in ink.

Fold and blot.

Add the details.

CHAPTER SIX

SWITZERLAND

On Boxing Day 1914 French, aged 60, left for Switzerland to raise money for the 'Waifs and Strays,' returning during February.

LINES IN A SWISS HOTEL (ANY OF THEM)

There's German in the music room,
There's French upon the stair,
There's English in the Grand Salon,
There's laughter everywhere.
The bunch from Boston hold their own
At every sort of noise,
Oh Switzerland! Oh Switzerland!
The land for healthy boys!

'We're off to bob,' 'We're off to ski,'
'We'll not be home till late.'
'A curling match - well after tea -
This morning I must skate.'
'Our trailing party starts at ten!'
And off to sport one whirls,
Oh Switzerland! Oh Switzerland!
The land for growing girls!

In leafy dells love weaves his spells
Where southern sunsets glow,
And hand in hand thro' fairyland
The lovers wander slow.
But hearts can throb on board a 'bob,'
We want no woodland glades.
Oh Switzerland! Oh Switzerland!
The land for men and maids!

Some day, old friend, I'd love to take
Our families and go
From London to Lucerne - and wake
Amid the sun and snow,
And see ourselves in joyous elves
(Our daughters and our sons,)
Oh Switzerland, Oh Switzerland!
The land for weary ones!

Ski jumping and after! St. Moritz.

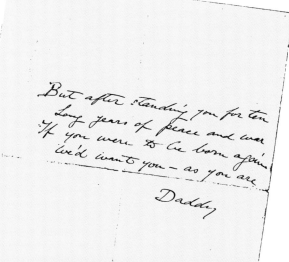

Lines written in praise of
Joan Phyllis French
A young lady who by
Constantly disregarding my
advice & eating more than
was good for her has
attained her eleventh year

Oh Joan when first you saw the light
you caused us much annoy,
For both your parents thought you might
as well have been a boy,

We had two daughters, each a gem
So thought — oh was it strange
We'd had about enough of them
— A boy would be a change

But after standing you for ten
Long years of peace and war
If you were to be born again
We'd want you — as you are

Daddy

Eventually the summer of 1914 saw Mollie and me in our first long frocks enjoying dances and a theatrical season that brought Nijinsky in ballet and Chaliapin in opera, and ended with a day at Henley. We were planning various future activities, including a trip to Switzerland for the winter sports, when the War put a stop to everything. Private entertainment disappeared, never to return.

(Ettie French)

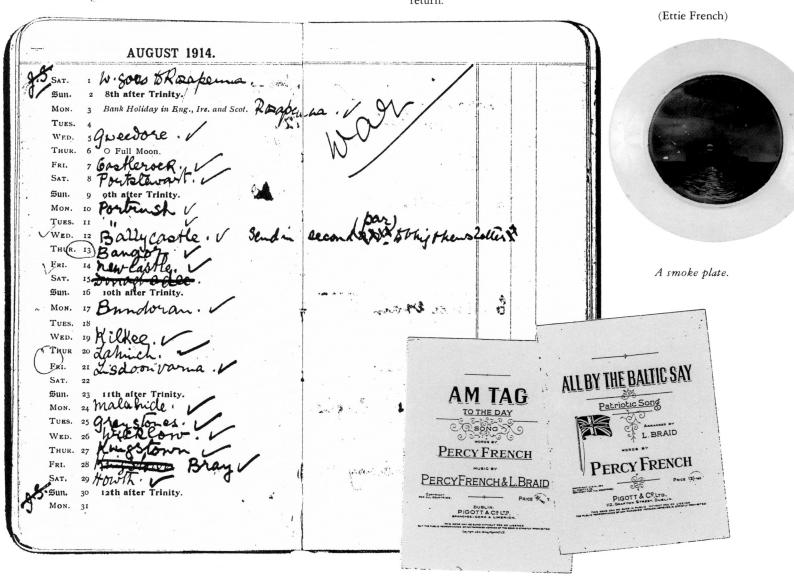

A smoke plate.

Portrait by Robert Ponsonby Staples.

LINES ON ETTIE'S 20th BIRTHDAY

Just twenty years ago was born
(Upon a most auspicious morn)
A little rose without a thorn
    Contented with her lot.

For though she had not form or rank
And not a penny in the bank
Or anything to make her swank
    It mattered not a jot.

She smiled upon her kith and kin
Who all responded with a grin.
Her work she took an interest in
    As well as in her play.

Some people think November 5
A date that one should keep alive
A memory that should survive
    As an eventful day.

But I would call November 4
A date we should rejoice at more
And joy bells ring from shore to shore
    On that auspicious morn.

For old grey bearded gaffers say
To tottering crones who pass that way
Just 20 years ago to-day
    Young Ettie French was born.

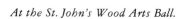

At the St. John's Wood Arts Ball.

A North Antrim Bog

As 'Michael O'Ryan,' the ballad singer.

Irish Life.

French with his nieces Maeve (front) and Daphne, sister Christina and brother Arthur (father of the girls.)

OUR FAVOURITE UNCLE

His first name being William, he was always known to us children as Uncle Willie, and was our favourite uncle. Looking back now on the years, my memories of his visits to us were of music and painting. Directly he arrived, out would come the banjo – later the guitar – and he would sing away, while we joined with gusto in the choruses. A table would then be cleared, and we would gather round while out came his paint-box and brushes, water, and a painting block. Giving us each a sheet of this and a paint-brush, he would show us first of all how to wet the surface all over with the paint-brush – not too much. Then we would start at the top, painting in the sky, blue, or if there was to be a burst of sunlight, up would go a thumb in the middle to mark, and remove, that much blue of sky! A range of mountains in the distance nearly always followed, with a bog, brown or heather covered – sometimes with a turf stack. Then a stream flowing down the centre, with a light at one point, reflecting the gleam from the sky, and made in the same way.

(Maeve Kenny, niece)

Few men have so many friends among all ranks of society as our genial humorist, Percy French. The English-speaking world knows him through his songs, the play-going public laugh with him as he stands on the platform telling us of " the lion that wouldn't eat parsley," or the adventures of " Carmody's mare," and the amateur water-colour painter tries vainly to copy " the mist that does be on Percy French's bog scenes." And now Ireland is glad to hear that the man who has been for many years the fountain-head of so much wholesome fun has not been forgotten amid this time of stress, for the Government have granted him an annuity which will go far to tide him over the troubled waters. Long may he live to enjoy this well-timed gift, for few men have given their services more freely in the cause of charity than he. Our photograph shows him and that admirable Irish comedienne, Miss Betty Duncan, in their new recital, " Lights and Shadows of Irish Life," with which they are now touring Ireland.

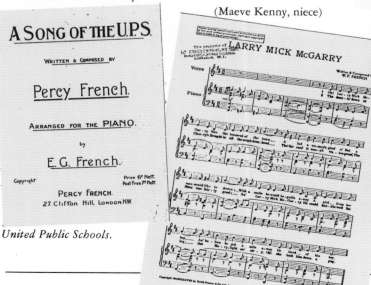

United Public Schools.

During the war years French worked with three different female stage partners.

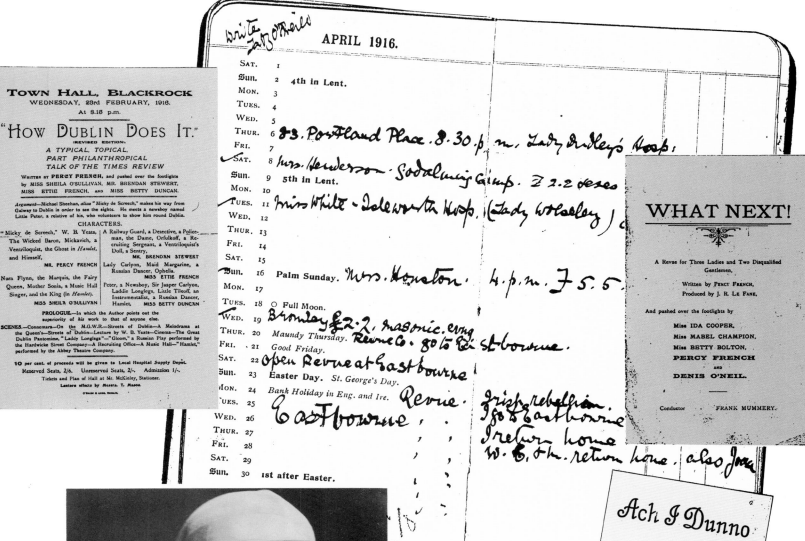

The Irish uprising of Easter 1916 abruptly disrupted his stage show.

Performing Carmody's Mare

From CARMODY'S MARE

There's the saddlin' bell ringing! - the numbers are up,
Oh, man dear! I must see the race for the Cup.
Push up on that plank there! hi! gimme a hand!
Oh, man! this is better than any Grand Stand.
There's high fliers payin' a shillin' - an' two
That hasn't the half, nor the quarter the view.
Hi! Peter! McGinty! Miginty me son
Come up here an' see the big race bein' run.
- Not room for another? Oh, now you be civil
- Come up here me haro! - An' you to the divil!
Look Peter from here you can see the whole Course
- Ay, call up a policeman, call up the whole Force!
There's the bank an' the hurdles an' there's the stone wall.
An' there's the big water jump, best o' them all.
Who am I backin'? Well, now I declare
I've got all me money on Carmody's mare!

THE KINDLY WELCOME

Ah! 'twill only be a shower,
Tho' the wind is from the west,
Just come in for half-an-hour
And give yerself a rest.

And was that what ye wor sketchin' –
Just the turf stack an' the whins?
And yer death o'cowld yer ketchin' –
Mary Ann, put out thim hins!

An' that picture, do ye say now
Ye could sell for thirty bob?
Still, this paintin' in a way now
Is a very lonesome job.

Oh! now yer welcome, honey,
To a little sup like that.
Is it be takin' money
For what wouldn't feed the cat!

Early in 1914, some months after I had come to Dublin, I was at a house dinner in the United Arts Club. This was an informal affair, and after dinner we had a sort of impromptu concert, at which anyone present might be called to assist. I was called on by the Hon. Secretary to give something of an 'enlivening' nature. Accordingly I moved to the piano and struck up Percy French's 'Phil the Fluter's Ball,' asking the company to join me in the chorus, which they did, and we finished with a riotous chorus. At the conclusion of the song, while there was tumultuous applause going on and calls for an encore, a quiet-looking grey-haired man came across to me and said 'Thank you so much, I've never heard my song sung better' – and to my astonishment I found I had been performing in the presence of Percy French himself. This interview resulted in my having the privilege and pleasure of helping Mr. French in public performances for about a year. Our joint performance as two old ballad singers, Micky the Screech and Biddy the Blackbird, singing *All by the Baltic Say* invariably brought down the house everywhere.

(Florence Marks)

With Florence Marks.

In the meantime French's previous stage partner, Betty Duncan, had moved into straight theatre. At her marriage on 27th November French read this tribute.

MEDITATIONS ON BETTY

I've seen her play in many parts,
And play them well – by fits and starts,
Once in the club they call 'The Arts'
She played a Pillar.

And when she sailed with me to France
The Captain never got a chance,
She swept the sea with eagle glance
And held the tiller.

Then, in my late Revue, we had
The humours of the Dublin lad,
And then she made Ophelia mad
As any hatter.

And when with me she winged her flight,
And faced the audience to recite
'Ach! I dunno,' 'twas always right,
No need to flatter.

But not alone the light of lime
Has seen her soar to height sublime,
Snowdonia knows how she can climb
Without assistance.

In pen and ink she might have made
A name, but people, I'm afraid,
Are still too fond of light and shade
And dreamy distance.

And now I find my lady wed,
A quiet wedding, be it said,
No slipper hit the bridegroom's head,
And no confetti.

And well she'll play this latest *role*
Supported by a kindred soul;
So, Comrades fill the flowing bowl!
I give you 'Betty!'

During the war French travelled to the Continent, entertaining the wounded in hospitals.

The Ghost of Ypres

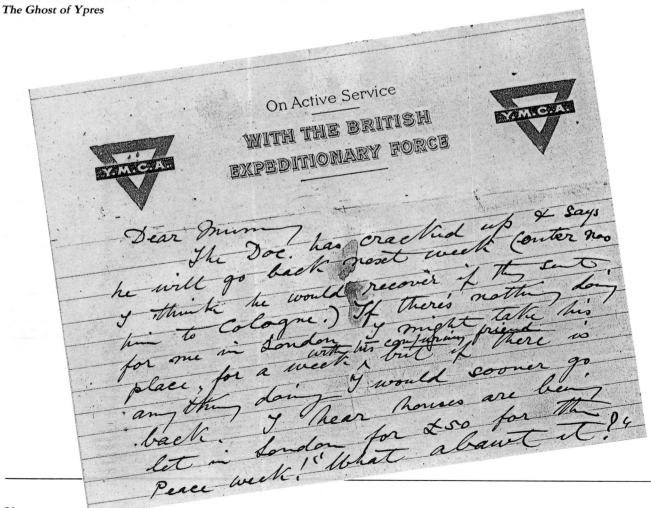

The Artist and the Colleen, with May Laffan.

A visit to Cloonyquin.

On the Erriff (County Galway)

KATEY RYAN

A sequel to The Emigrant's Letter

Oh girls there's come a letter
From the boy who sailed away
Two years ago an' better
To the land beyond the say.
Pat Malone has made his forchin,
We're to meet him on the strand
For across the say he's marchin'
To the ould Town land!

To the ould Town land!
'Tis as if a fairy wand
Had doubled all the sunshine
In the ould Town land!

He's to build a house and slate it
For he says he's made his pile,
An' 'twill all be decorated
In the very best of style.
There'll be an upper storey,
All the boys will lend a hand
Till it rises in its glory
In the ould Town land.

In the ould Town land –
With a garden understand –
There won't be such another
In the ould Town land!

There's a postscrip' to the letter
That is lyin' next me heart,
And I like that bit the better
Than all the other part.
P.S. Tell Katey Ryan
'Tis the house for her I planned
Since the day I left her cryin'
In the ould Town land.

In the ould Town land,
Oh don't you understand
I'm the only Katey Ryan
In the whole Town land.

The French silver wedding was on 24 Jan.

1894 ———— 1919

*If we had lived upon our lone
and never married - Golly
By now an ancient cat I'd own
and you a pretty Polly
But such a course I think we've shown
Had been surpassing folly
For where would Ettie be! and Joan!
and need I mention Mollie!*

W. P. to H. M. C.

STEINWAY HALL

There is something quite enticing in the legend " Humours of Art and Music," applied to the entertainment in which Mr. Percy French and Mr. Sterndale Bennett are to be seen and heard every afternoon this week at Steinway Hall. And the title proves no misnomer. For the best part of two hours the humours of Mr. French at his easel and Mr. Bennett at his piano kept their audience well amused, and what more could mortal demand of any entertainers? London, of course, long since discovered that the artist first-named can do surprisingly clever things with his chalks and his charcoal. His methods are not precisely those adopted by every artist. For instance, he sometimes elects to execute his drawing upside down. In this manner yesterday afternoon Mr. French, before the astonished eyes of his audience, deftly fashioned a seascape. At another moment, with lightning rapidity, he illustrated a " Tale of Two Lovers " as it was unfolded in song by his companion, while at another the two humorists set themselves to improvise upon a theme of a couple of words suggested in the auditorium. Mr. Bennett, for his part, sang to his own accompaniment some blithe little songs, of which the best—one called " Life in the Country "—combines the virtues of pointed words and a taking tune. He also addressed himself to the amiable task of repairing the deficiencies of his hearers' musical knowledge by giving them the " History of Song "—" from the far-away chimes of pre-Adamite times to the modern crimes of pantomimes." " Why one should marry an orphan " was the peremptory title of Messrs. French and Bennett's finale, and it can only have been reprehensible moral cowardice awakened in them by such a title that induced some male members of the audience to leave before that item in the varied programme was reached.

In Suffolk.

Signature for a passport application, December 1919. Further trips to Switzerland were planned.

LATER ON

When we're children at our lessons, it is beautiful to think
Of the good time that is coming later on,
When we've done with silly copy-books and horrid pens and ink,
What a lovely time is coming later on!
The rivers of New Zealand, the mountains of Peru,
The watersheds of Europe, and the tribes of Timbuctoo,
All the facts without the fancies, all the tiresome and the true,
Will be nowhere in that lovely later on.

We'll forget the foolish fables that were written by Fontaine,
In the pleasant time that's coming later on,
At those twelve times twenty tables we will never look again,
In the lazy time that's coming later on.
The date of Magna Charta, the plot they called 'the Rye,'
The counties that are bounded by the Humber and the Wye,
We may not quite forget them, but we mean to have a try
In the lazy time that's coming later on.

Oh my optimistic hero, there are lessons you must learn,
In the queer time that is coming later on,
And masters and examiners you'll find at every turn,
In the hard times that are coming later on.
Miss Fortune is a governess who'll teach you many things,
A tutor called Experience will moderate your flings,
You'll learn how men make money, and you'll learn that it has wings,
In the strange times that are coming later on.

Then you'll meet the radiant Vision who is all the world to you,
(You'll attend her mother's lectures later on,)
You'll learn that what's enough for one is not enough for two,
Nor enough for half a dozen later on.
No, the work is never ended, though for holidays you crave,
There are pop-guns to be mended for the Robbers in the Cave.
You fancy you're the master, but you find that you're a slave
To a curly headed tyrant later on.

And so through all your lifetime you are longing for the day,
The lovely day that's coming later on,
When pens and ink and copy-books will all be laid away,
And that day is surely coming later on.
For when you're really tired, having done your level best,
When the story's nearly ended, and the sun sets in the west,
Then you'll lie down very gently, and the weary will find rest,
And I fancy we'll deserve it - later on.

Later on, later on,
Oh so many friends have gone,
Sweet lips that smiled and loving eyes that shone.
Through the darknesss into light,
One by one they've winged their flight,
Perhaps we'll play together - later on.

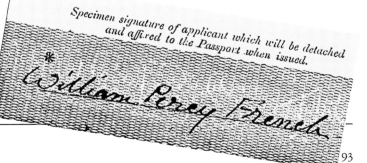

Specimen signature of applicant which will be detached and affixed to the Passport when issued.

William Percy French

Chalk drawing by Sheila Coffey.

French's final engagement was in Glasgow. Afterwards, in failing health, he called at Formby with his cousin, Canon Richardson.

With May Laffan

THE PALETTE CLUB LIMITED,
GLASGOW.
FRIDAY EVENING, 16th JANUARY, 1920, at 7-45 p.m.

ARTISTS:

MR. ALFRED O'SHEA	TENOR
CAPTAIN MACLAGAN BLAIR	BASS
MISS FLORENCE MACBRIDE	SOLO VIOLIN
MR. CROSSLAND HIRST	AT THE PIANO

AND

MR. PERCY FRENCH and MISS MAY LA FAN in Song, Story, Chalk and Banjo Solos.

PROGRAMME.

Mr. Alfred O'Shea	"Donna non vidi mai" (Manon Lescaut)	Puccini
Miss Florence MacBride	{ (a) "Cherry Ripe" ... ... { (b) "Chinese Melodies"	Cyril Scott Kreisler
Captain MacLagan Blair	"When a maiden takes your fancy" (Il Seraglio) ...	Mozart
Mr. Percy French and Miss May La Fan	{ "In the Tropics" ... ... { A Chalk chuckle (The origin of Man, Woman and Boy) { Banjo Solo—"The Darktown Dandies"	

Interval of 25 minutes

Gentlemen will greatly oblige by going up to the Smoking Room as speedily as possible,
to facilitate the serving of tea to the Ladies in Concert Hall.

Mr. Percy French and Miss May La Fan	{ A Lapse into Literature ... ... { (Doomed to the dust bin, and Beauty and the Bunker) { Coon Song—"The Hoodoo" (Illustrated)	
Mr. Alfred O'Shea	"The snowy breasted pearl"	Robinson
Captain MacLagan Blair	{ (a) "The hour of sleep" ... ... { (b) "Youth"	Lambert Francis Allitson Gossec
Miss Florence MacBride	{ (a) "Mazurka" ... ... { (b) "Scottish Melodies"	
Mr. Alfred O'Shea	{ (a) "In a Garden" ... ... { (b) "Two eyes of brown"	Hawley Cowen
Captain MacLagan Blair	"Onaway, awake"	
Mr. Percy French and Miss May La Fan	{ Duet—"In quest of the quiet" ... ... { An episode in the life of Little Willie { and "That Children's Party" ... ... { Sketch—"The letter from the Front"	

A Limited number of Tickets still on hand for
FREDERICK DAWSON'S PIANOFORTE LECTURE RECITAL
or
CATTERALL STRING QUARTET.

COMPOSED IN BED.
By W. P. F.

Aunt Mary Anne, Aunt Mary Anne,
The Sole Survivor of the Clan,
Who laughed, and danced, and romped, and
ran

In dear old Clooniquin !
I write these lines when in my bed,
Whereon I lay my weary head,
Exhausted, sick; but not **quite** dead,
And hardly worth a pin.

Yet on thy Birthday I must see
Can I not send a Rhyme to thee,
Whose thoughts so often are with me:
And therefore I would say,
Dear Aunt, your love has been to me,
So cheery in my misery,
We all send hope that we may see
You with us many a day.

The last poem, written on 21st January for the 97th birthday of his favourite aunt, and later published in the church magazine.

*French died from pneumonia on 24 January at Formby, aged 65. He is buried there in St. Luke's churchyard. Lines from his favourite hymn, **Lead Kindly Light**, are engraved on his tombstone: O'er moor and fen, o'er crag and torrent, till the night is gone.*

DEATH OF MR. PERCY FRENCH.

The announcement of the death of Mr. Percy French, which occurred on Saturday at the house of a friend in Liverpool, will be received with feelings of deep regret by all to whom his entertainments afforded unalloyed pleasure throughout the United Kingdom. His health had been failing for some time past, and eventually pneumonia developed and proved fatal. Mr. French was the second son of Mr. Christopher French, D.L., of Cloonaquin, Co. Roscommon. He was a graduate of Trinity College, and for some years practised the profession of engineer; but his tastes lay in another direction, and gradually he adopted the profession of public entertainer. He had a fund of quiet humour which found an appropriate outlet in his sketches and songs. The songs which formed part of his entertainment were all of his own composition, and some of them, such as "The Mountains of Mourne," are likely to be popular for many years to come. The vocal portion of his entertainment was invariably taken by Mr. French himself, and while he sang he played the banjo as an accompaniment. It was a testimony to his versatile attainments that, without any other aid than that of a lady who presided at the piano, he could hold for two hours the undivided attention of his patrons. He was disposed occasionally to satirise different classes of society, but it was done in a humorous way, creating only amusement without causing bitterness or resentment. Mr. French was not only a writer of excellent verse, but he was also noted as a lightning cartoonist and water-colour artist. He painted a series of Irish landscapes for the late King Edward, by whom they were much appreciated. A regular contributor to which his last a parody on as a pensioner to married, and leav

IRISH ENTERTAINER'S DEATH.

Mr. Percy French, the entertainer, who died at Liverpool recently, belonged to a well-known Irish family. He was educated at Trinity College, Dublin, and took the engineering degree, but soon turned to the profession of platform entertainer. He rendered his humorous Irish songs all over the British Isles and in America, being accompanied on many of his tours by Dr. Houston Collisson, the clergyman-musician. Mr. French's character sketches—especially the Irish—were inimitable. He turned his knowledge of art to account in lightning sketching on the platform, often combining singing and sketching in a single "act." He will be missed by a large circle of friends.

Silhouette by Hubert Leslie.

DEATH OF MR. PERCY FRENCH

A FAMOUS IRISH ENTERTAINER.

Mr. Percy French died at the house of his friend in Liverpool on Saturday, in his 66th year.

The late Mr. French was the son of Mr. C. French, D.L., Cloonaquin, Co. Roscommon. After graduating at Trinity College he practised for some time as an engineer. We next find him as editor of "The Irish Jarvey," a comic paper which ran two years, and from this period of his life he obtained material for one of his sketches "How I Ran My Magazine." He next came forward as a playwright and actor. He played in "The Knight of the Road," the music of which was written by Dr. Collison. Another opera, "Strongbow," as Mr. French chose a period of history which was not congenial to national sentiment.

INIMITABLE SKETCHES.

It was after this that Mr. French hit upon the form of entertainment which won him a world-wide reputation. His inimitable sketches brimful of wholesome and genuine humour drew large audiences in all parts of the United Kingdom. He gained considerable distinction as a song writer, the most notable including "Phil, the Fluter's Ball," and "Where the Mountains of Mourne Sweep Down to the Sea," and "Are Ye Right There, Michael?" As early as 1893 he exhibited water colours in the Dublin Academy.

Mr. Percy French.

DEATH OF MR. PERCY FRENCH.

AN A
(From a

The death of Per shock not only to t sonal friends, to w humour, his gay and deared him, but to friends who were his uncommon gift of maki he entertained; they in a moment. The di his to give, and his w bitterness. A true lo delicate humour never j tive, in a land where s approaching ridicule has His audiences realised t the gentle mockery of a a well-beloved mistress. comedy breathes from h and original turns of phra mosphere have made them of the world where Irish gether.

There are few men to excel in more than one for French was the exception to people will think of him i colour painter of rare char ferred painting to writing pression, and he was never l with his brushes and colour memory of the light break hills with a stretch of bogl ground, or of a lonely seas covered rocks, round which tl Slight as are many of these s imbued with something of the he loved. His painting, no less was inspired by a deep affectio

OBITUARY.

MR. PERCY FRENCH.

The innumerable audiences to whom he gave such pleasure will regret to learn that Mr. Percy French, the well-known entertainer, died on Tuesday. A graduate of Trinity College, Dublin, he was, in his younger days, a civil engineer, but it was his work as an entertainer that will keep his memory green. A correspondent who knew him writes: To those who knew Percy French at all intimately it would be difficult indeed to conceive a more lovable man. He died at his work, as he would have wished to die, and those of us who knew him well will feel assured that he faced death with a fortitude strengthened by that gaiety of spirit which was inseparable from all that was so irresistibly Percy French. He was approaching his 70th year, but he had lost nothing of his zest in life. He had crammed every moment with an intense effort to give encouragement and amusement to the people with whom he came into contact. During the war he must have lessened the anguish and quickened the weary hours of innumerable soldiers laid aside in our hospitals; and into barracks and camps he also took his brave outlook and the invincible spirit of his humour. There was no more popular entertainer at schools and colleges than he, and to see him in an audience of schoolboys or an audience of the youngest children was a pleasure difficult to rate.

Death of Well-known Composer

POPULAR ENTERTAINER

Some Reminiscences

The news of the death of Mr. Percy French, the Irish composer and entertainer, which took place in Liverpool on Saturday, will be heard with regret in the Irish capital by a host of personal friends and by the public generally, who knew him as an entertainer.

Mr. French had been unwell for some time, and passed away at the house of a friend in the Mersey city.

Mr. Percy French was the second son of the late Mr. Christopher French, of Cloonyquin, Co. Roscommon. His eldest brother, Major French, who succeeded to the family estates, was a major in the Royal Artillery, and at the outbreak of the Boer War, and again in 1914, rejoined the army.

Mr. Percy French received his early education at Windermere College, from which he entered the University of Dublin. He took his degree in the ordinary course, adopting civil engineering as his profession. In 1876 he obtained employment as an inspector of some drainage works in the County Cavan. This position he held for six years, when he finally gave up engineering and turned to literature and art as a means of livelihood. He composed a number of songs, which took the public taste immediately. The first of these was "Abdallah, Balbul Ameer," which was soon heard in every barrack room in the army, and became widely popular in all circles of society. This song made his fame, but through omitting to copyright it, he pecuniary profit, as it was Percy French's in the field of broad not the mastery of verse possessed by either Mr. or Mr. James Lowry, but as laughter-producing as himself, who would have the skit entitled Queen after supper at the Vice-ported by Timothy Finegan,

some people said," sez she, atly in dread, sez she, ured and sot sez she, ot, sez she; ear, sez she; here, sez she; in' hearts, sez she, he well, sez she, Parnell, sez she er wan, sez she, tonne, sez she, black, sez she, ne back, sez she; care, sez she, wear, sez she; bare, sez she; re, sez she. there's a slate, sez she, eats, sez she, e crimes, sez she, in the "Irish Times," sez she."

Postscript:

Mollie and Lennie died in 1956.

Cloonyquin House, 48 Springfield Road and 27 Clifton Hill no longer exist.

49 Middle Abbey Street was burnt down in 1929 and rebuilt.

The Old Curiosity Shop has long since disappeared.

The end of the holiday

WATERCOLOURS REPRODUCED IN THIS BOOK

For the loan of paintings thanks are due to Derek Collie, Ettie and Joan French, John Gough, Courtney Kenny, Maeve Kenny, The Oriel Gallery, The Percy French Society, Oscar Rollins, Kay Saunders, John Stewart, Trinity College Dublin and the Ulster Museum.

Places in Ireland where French is known
to have performed.

Abbeyleix, Antrim, Ardglass, Armagh, Athboy, Athenry, Athlone, Athy, Avoca.

Bagenalstown, Bailieborough, Balbriggan, Ballaghaderreen, Ballina, Ballinamore, Ballinasloe, Ballinrobe, Ballybay, Ballybunion, Ballycastle, Ballymahon, Ballymoney, Ballymote, Ballyshannon, Banbridge, Bandon, Bangor, Belfast, Beltra, Belturbet, Birr, Blackrock, Blarney, Boyle, Bray, Buncrana, Bundoran, Buttevant.

Cahir, Carlow, Carrickfergus, Carrickmacross, Carrick-on-Shannon, Carrick-on-Suir, Castlebar, Castleblaney, Castleknock, Castlepollard, Castlereagh, Castlerock, Castletownshend, Cavan, Claremorris, Clones, Clongowes, Clonmel, Clontarf, Cloonyquin, Coleraine, Collooney, Cookstown, Cootehill, Cork.

Dalkey, Derry, Donaghadee, Donegal, Downpatrick, Drogheda, Drumcondra, Dublin, Dundalk, Dundrum, Dungannon, Dungarvan, Dungiven, Dunlavin, Dunmore.

Edenderry, Ennis, Enniscorthy, Enniskillen, Ennistymon.

Fermoy, Fintona.

Galway, Glaslough, Gorey, Gort, Greystones, Gweedore.

Holywood, Howth.

Kells, Kildare, Kilkee, Kilkeel, Kilkenny, Killarney, Kilrush, Kingstown (now Dun Laoghaire), Kinsale.

Lahinch, Larne, Letterkenny, Limavady, Limerick, Lisdoonvarna, Lismore, Listowel, Longford, Loughrea, Lucan, Lurgan.

Macroom, Magherafelt, Malahide, Mallow, Manorhamilton, Maryborough, Midleton, Mohill, Monaghan, Moy, Mullarany, Mullingar.

Naas, Navan, Nenagh, Newbridge, Newcastle, New Ross, Newtownabbey, Newtownstewart.

Oldcastle, Omagh.

Parknasilla, Pilborough, Portaferry, Portarlington, Portora, Portrush, Portsalon, Portstewart, Punchestown.

Queenstown (now Cobh.)

Randalstown, Rathdowney, Rosapenna, Roscommon, Roscrea, Rosses Point.

Salthill, Sandymount, Skerries, Skibbereen, Sligo, Strabane, Strangford, Swinford.

Tandragee, Thomastown, Thurles, Tipperary, Tralee, Tramore, Trim, Tuam, Tubbercurry, Tullamore.

Warrenpoint, Waterford, Westport, Wexford, Whitehead, Wicklow.

Youghal.

INDEX OF WORKS

FURTHER READING

The Jarvey. . . . . edited by W. P. French . . . . Dublin 1889-90
  (complete edition in National Library of Ireland)
Handbook of the Irish Parliament Houses. . . . . H. Goldsmith Whitton . . . . Alex Thom 1891
  illustrated by Mrs. Ethel French
Dr. Collisson in and on Ireland . . . . W. A. Houston Collisson . . . . Robert Sutton
Chronicles of Percy French . . . . Mrs. de Burgh Daly . . . . Talbot Press 1922
The years of my pilgrimage. . . . . John Ross . . . . London 1924
Pilgrim Scrip . . . . Sir John Ross . . . . London 1927
Songs of Percy French, vols 1 & 2. . . . . Keith Prowse
The Irish Troubadour (More Songs of Percy French) . . . . Keith Prowse
Percy French and his songs . . . . James N. Healy . . . . Mercier Press 1966
The World of Percy French . . . . Brendan O'Dowda . . . . Blackstaff Press 1981
The Songs of Percy French . . . . James N. Healy . . . . Mercier Press 1983

The Mountains o' Mourne.